Pilgrim's Gait

DAVID CRAIG

RESOURCE *Publications* • Eugene, Oregon

PILGRIM'S GAIT

Resource Publications
An Imprint of Wipf and Stock Publishers
199 W. 8th Ave., Suite 3
Eugene, OR 97401

www.wipfandstock.com

ISBN 13: 978-1-4982-2556-4

Manufactured in the U.S.A. 05/07/2015

For the ones I have failed too often:
Linda, David, Bridget, and Jude

Contents

Pilgrim Places

"Moment of Conscience"

—Garabandal

1.
San Vicente de la Barquera: boat beached
in mid-river sand—the Catholic in Europe!
Not everything-in-its-Puritan-place;
but the thing, skewed, as place.

Garabandal grows out of the Cantabrians,
buildings squatting in irregular red stone, mortar—
though everyone we met was from somewhere else.
I felt like the Beach Boys, waiting for a wave:
"the moment of conscience," with a woman
someone knew who'd married a brother
of one of the visionaries!

(It was labor intensive,
this waiting for God!)

I got to stand—the pillar said—where St. Michael
had stood! And later, as we prayed our rosaries
beneath the pines, hoping for the three o'clock
change: strange swirls of low grey clouds appeared,
God finger-painting, moving them
under higher slate; a whole new world
seemed in the offing.

(Jude, for his three year old Downs' part,
chimed in with comedic "alleluias.")

The appointed hour: nothing happened!

Nothing.

Wrong year.

2.
Many of those pilgrims dead now: sunny Erla,
wigged switch board operator—cancer;
a too-needy Frank, on his crutches; both with what
Fr. Peter had labeled "real problems."

And he was almost right. Jude is life-raft,
yes. Who's ever been happier just to run,
as awkward as time, though his pain
is real enough, seventeen years later:
never finding a face to suit his classmates,
or a girlfriend, or a talent in life.

I caught a soccer game, passing a bar:
their Monday Night football; and huge,
beautiful statues, two over-sized religious stores;
our theologian and his family
seeming to go to confession every hour
as the time neared.

I ran into Fr. Scadron—ex-Parisian
artist, Jew—the priest my wife
had just edited a book for.

(I wondered if he were real!)

The locals were used to it, the us of things:
one Garabandal woman, hanging laundry
as Jude played with her boy's trucks in the dust,
me sitting on a nearby stone
next to an older Dutch guy, a man who knew
the minutiae of every apparition
everywhere—trying to situate himself
in the infinite know.

It was all anti-climax, which was only right—
because our lives are precisely that.
Each one brought Jesus with him to get there,
shared Him along the way. And though I know
Jude, seventeen years later, would still like
to be healed—to have a life like other people,
what could any of us, finally, have traded
for what we'd been given?

Lourdes

After French McDonald's,
an older, thicker bicyclist—with curls—
not yet pathetic, lagged behind, racing
younger mates. I watched him,
Jude on my shoulders. (We sized each other:
France and America, in the wake
of Charles de Gaulle.)

Just outside the gates of that heaven,
that idyll of praise: shops stuffed the street,
good art—and not—for sale.

Tasteful French corps pushed wheelchairs
inside; and underground, a massive church,
like some holy bus terminal: 100,000 people;
Masses, screens in different languages—
the great, decaying church up top, with its inclines,
pews, decrepit enough to convince anyone
that what mattered most wasn't there.

In town at Sacred Heart Church,
where the actor-priest had reduced Bernadette
to sainthood: no pews, just benches
and the Mass in French—airy as a town square,
which is what it was: the nation's fiber.

Pilgrim's Gait

Jude, at three, ran across that basement,
through shadows, just to sit next to
a darkened statue of St. John Vianney.

The water in the holy baths froze,
and I, flippant: tasteless at mom's, bouncing
on her furniture—as an attendant mumbled
something about reverence.

We both caught colds.

The Santa Fe Staircase (Tour)

Next to a large diocesan bookstore
grab, a decommissioned Loretto;
you couldn't walk up the tight circular—
car vibrations! (Everything truly good
gets lost: the depth, prayer which sustains.)

Thirty-three steps, a novena's answer
to bad carpentry!

I try to picture St. Joseph in a saddle.
Eastwood's cigar, Mexican poncho, a level
in his holster. He bent the wood in water,
just down the road from Georgia O'Keefe's museum.

I went to see a nearby church with holy dirt:
El Santuario de Chimayo. (Humble locals
were worried about its lean, as we waited—
like one must, it seems, at every site.)

A small room contained a round pit,
the "holy dirt," adjacent Prayer Room
with photos, all the crutches you could use.
People ate the soil, back when they had no shame,
nothing to lose.

Theirs are the crutches!

I took some home in a vial.

The cliff dwellings nearby were different:
ruins of pueblos. Ladders and drawings,
worn stone steps. God dancing, as He always does,
in feathers, in the past—It's where we see Him best.

How sweet and dry the American West is:
blue sky, scrubbing brush, canyons,
the smooth run of car wheels.

Fake Apparition

—in Carrollton, OH

The theologian's old Victorian sunroom
windows—stack of locutions on the sill.
Having been appointed by the Bishop,
he just shook his head.

We went out to play hoops with his kids:
side yard, cracked asphalt, full court.

He'd built a monastery, because a change
is coming: huge dormitories, beautiful church—
Mark's ark, I kidded him, still empty
for the most part, just a few religious
in a new order. But the gesture!
It was rich: like our lives, what we hope to fill—
Francis's fools!

Do it again! Do it again!

Let our hearts be the flagstone
everyone walks on!

As a young family, ours used to follow his
around Hopedale's Sacred Heart Church,
Eucharistic procession. Absurd Catholics,

dressing up the present in banners, deacon's garb,
as if we know what gives it expression!

How many heroes we've known!

Bounce the ball, young one.
Bounce the ball.

Oil for the Turn

The Madonna's House

1.

Within the week I was on a muzzled Greyhound, heading into the Great White North—Canady. Destination: Moose Jaw, Ontario. I waved good-bye to my All-American college life, hugs for everyone. Both Israel and Periwinkle wished me happy trails. She patted me on the back, congratulated me for having escaped the blight of intellectualism and suburbia; Israel suggesting that, when in a squeeze, running away is certainly an option. Then he grinned, shook my hand, told me to keep a record.

And there I was, on a bus, duffel bag stuffed with clothes and books, bad money, playing out my options in my head. How, I wondered, was I going to convince these people that I was in earnest about their religion without sounding like the complete phony I was. Maybe some choked reticence? A kind of constant, tacit, respectably distant fawn? The Gollum slither? I was good at that. Maybe just keep my mouth shut for a change. Now that would be a miracle. Besides, who knew, maybe I might even find Anita Bryant in the process.

But there was more to it than flight, I had to admit that to myself as well. This whole God bidness—evangelical Okie t.v., the money tree. I wanted to check it out, had for awhile. I'd read the GITA, some Rilke, had even spent time arguing with Jesus people at the university.

If there was something there, I wanted to know.

(Six degrees of suck was no way to go through life.)

I looked for the Falls when we got to Buffalo, never saw them. It was funny, I had always complained about America. But now that I was leaving my Bizarro-world home, I had mixed feelings. Would I be back? I thought back to the Ohio, brown enough to walk across. Still, it could sparkle sometimes in the afternoon sun, and when spring came, there was this nice light green that worked its way up the surrounding, polluted hills. I remembered all the rednecks at CJ's, Linden's as well, nobody at either place giving a damn about anything except what they had going on in front of them.

That was bully America, but if it walked loudly, carried a big stick, it was a blindness I at least felt comfortable with. This Canada thing would be a whole different slot machine.

I didn't have too much trouble at the border, wore all new clothes, creases to facilitate my crossing: some new Levis, a lumberjack shirt, a pair of light leather work boots. I even sported a haircut. I tried to keep things light and moving by talking retreat to the guard in front of me, a month long exercise, I told him, in deep breathing. Slowing down, that's where it was at. I jabbered away, told him I was taking a month off from my job, advised him to stash every penny of his retirement fund into the stock market. Keep talking, I said to myself as he had me begin to unload my bag.

More shirts, brand new heavy socks, thermal shorts. All of it, just out of the wrapper, two dress shirts with pins still in them. Was it all too much, I wondered? Apparently not, because he let me through. Maybe he just got tired of hearing my impersonation. Whatever, I decided. Things could have gotten difficult had we worked our way down to the dour roll of bills.

"Have a nice day, EH?" I said with a wink.

He waved me on, smiling at the cliché. "Take off."

Toronto was cleaner than I thought possible for a big city. The guard rails on the sides of the interprovince coming in were not banged up; there was no flying debris, no dust working the support posts, no overgrown weeds along the sides of the highways either. And yet the place didn't have the Puritan feel of America. What made these boys tick, I wondered? I had never been to Britain, so I couldn't really see how much of an effect it had. "Keep Britain tidy," I guessed that worked here as well.

And what exactly was a Commonwealth I wondered? A loose confederacy of nations. Share a queen. (Another "Bloody" Elizabeth, every queen since the renaissance, in some way, virgin?) The whole thing struck me as being slightly geeky. What exactly did they expect to get from old marble-bottom anyway? Wisdom? Certainly not her caish. Inspiration perhaps, a sense of who they were?

Oh, Canada, tidy Canada, what bugs are up thy shorts, I wondered? I'd have to sit back in this alien nation I finally decided, that much was clear. Let the robot do the talking.

Everyone was so pleasant. It made for suspicion. The bus drivers looked like nicer versions of Chicago policemen, with their checkered Blue Line Voyager hats. Daley would have rolled over on his graves. I wouldn't have wished America on anyone, even then, but at first this place gave me the heebie-jeebies. It was way too neat.

The bus station in Toronto was a two-level job, more like a travel agency than a bus terminal. Sculpted concrete, nice, if few, seats. No loiterers here I guessed. Everyone had direction in Canada, or were encouraged to have some. It made me laugh, the imaginative stretch it would have taken to get the uninformed, an Eskimo say, to believe that this place was of the same genre as the Port Authority in New York—or the Greyhound Station in Cleveland for that matter—where every scab-infected unfortunate on the earth pitches a tent in front of the t.v.'s, hits you up for a buck, giving you t.b. in the process.

It didn't look like diseases were allowed in Canada. But how had they managed it? Socialized medicine? Cold northern virtue? Maybe the whole country wears a wig. It's respectability, denial. Keep your sins at home. We just don't do that here. And all the while, beneath that veil, giving license to every "progressive" notion of victimhood. As much as they say they detest American chest-pounding, they fall in line.

By the time the bus had gotten to Peterborough, I was about ready to jump ship. Just what was I doing up here? I didn't even remember the basic tenants of the Catholic faith. Wasn't one supposed to do something when going into a church? Sprinkle himself with holy water or kiss, worship at the feet of Mary goddess? Why hadn't I paid more attention? What if I gave myself away, made some accurate comment?

My anxiety waned, though, as I did a quick hike around part of the town to stretch my legs during the rest stop. Quaint. What were these nice, clean Canadian Catholics going to do to me anyway, throw me to Canadian lions? To Bert Lahrs . . . fur brekfesst?

Peterborough was clean as a spitless whistle. All the funny money, the slightly taciturn, if smiling, folk. I wondered what the insane asylums looked like up here. No need for straight jackets. Just tell the inmates to sit here, go there. Or if they did have jackets on, you could watch them skinny along the ground, humping like cartoon worms, cocoons, obeying your every command. I wondered if they had a test to tell who the insane ones were? Or did they just march up, confess it meekly. "I'm insane, you know. It's true. I have a paper right here." In crayon, big tears.

After a quick look through a liquor store, more like a supermarket with rollers than the institutional look you get back in the states, I bought a bigger bag of M & Ms, headed back to the bus. I felt so good that I even talked to some old lady awhile as we rolled up the perfect highway, ever northward.

It got old, the ride. Moose Jaw was a long way. I wondered if they had running water, any summer to speak of up there. I'd find out soon enough, and as late afternoon waned, chilled, I tried to make a bed of the seat. In snatches I watched what looked like virgin forest pass by: more and more birch, pine, fir. Too neat, way too neat.

We stopped for dinner at a restaurant. Kind of a cleaned-up Nebraska, with corn-fed proprietors, friendly, gabby in a local sort of way. The woman behind the register and the driver were old buds I guessed, everyone with that often higher pitched Canadian way of speaking. There was an awful rightness to this place as well, nicely creased napkins and spotless water glasses because it was a place to eat. A fresh bulletin board with notices about Moose Lodge meetings, boy-scout camperees. Not one whiff of dope, unkempt facial hair. I would not take up bowling I decided. They couldn't make me.

When I finished my cheeseburger, the cheese squarely on top of meat, placed perfectly below the bun, I stepped outside, finally noticed the snow that had put the squeeze in their voices. It was piled high along the edges of the parking lot. It wasn't terribly cold, but I had miscalculated. Spring up here was not running on the same schedule as in Ohio. I would need a winter coat. No stores between here and Moose Jaw either I bet.

2.

I was the only one to get out at my stop, hours later. The driver followed me down, flipped up the underneath compartment door and got me my duffel bag without a word. That was it. Just me and the exhaust, in the middle of a new world. The mooses. (I called a few times, no answer.)

Looking at the size of the town, rubbing up my creased jacket sleeves, I was surprised it was on the map at all. On my side of the street there was a red barn-shaped general store behind me. Clean, neat. It's competition, a Western front, two doors down on the same side, the post office/restaurant in between. The only other building on this side was a rent-all place some 400 yards—a-hem—meters down the road. On the other side of the street, a laundromat and a very small motel, closed for the season. There was a docking ramp out back for what I was to learn was the Madawaska River. Apparently tourists liked this place in the summer.

The river behind the motel was beautiful: wide, surrounded by miles and miles of dense forest, the salt of birch, a mild confusion in the branches. That was it, though, as far as the city was concerned. No sidewalks. Just sand by the road. I stood out there for awhile in the dark, getting cold, wondering just what my next move should be. It was never made clear to me over the phone where exactly the farm was in relation to the highway, or where I was to be picked up for that matter. I hadn't asked: so I had no choice right then but to stand there, befuddled in my mint new latest things, banks of snow shoveled, eye level on either side of the restaurant.

Finally, I just sat down on my duffel bag, in front of my repeating breath. After a while I decided. I'd just have to go across the street, find the house behind that motel and knock.

I didn't even have time to reach down and pick up my bag, though, because a van pulled around in front of me, up to the post office next door. Some guy got out and deposited a slew of mail into the all-night slot before spotting me. I figured he must be the guy, given the volume, and walked over. "Are you looking for The Madonna's Farm," he asked? "Nobody told me anybody was corning."

Given the obvious organization, I figured I was in for a treat. Who ran the place, a bunch of old, burnt-out hippies?

"I have," I said grandly (going for early humor), but it was like he didn't even hear me.

"And jeepers, no winter coat. Come prepared, eh? You could've frozen out here. Hop in." He had a fine Irish brogue, youngish. About thirty or so, with a long reddish beard. (He looked like one of the Smith Brothers.)

"Got any cough drops," I asked him?

"You like it, eh," he asked, laughing like a leprechaun, pulling down on his whiskers? "It's a gift from me old grandmother. I wonder why no one told me someone was coming?"

"God will take care of me," I ventured.

"Indeed. But a fine winter coat wouldn't hurt any, either, now would it? Well, best be getting back," he said with a laugh. The van was bare bones, a second seat behind ours, hinged benches along the back panels which served as flip-top containers. After a pause he added, "Welcome to The Madonna's Farm." He turned and bowed. "My namc is Patrick, and I will be your flight attendant. How did you hear about us, anyway?" I told him about the

Newman Center, said I needed to find my way, within the context of the Catholic faith, of course.

"We can lend you a coat tonight. Tomorrow's a half-day. You can go up to St. Joe's in the afternoon. You'll be able to pick up something cheaply."

"Great, cheap and free, two magic words as far as I'm concerned." He didn't answer, so I wondered if I had been too flippant, decided to heel the hounds. We drove that way, him only breaking the silence to point out St. Joseph's Rural Outreach Center, which we passed on our way in.

As we pulled into the gravel parking lot, I got my first glimpse of the main house. It was an old well-kept, steep-roofed white house off to the right side of the lot. And judging by how well lit the first floor was, it looked like things were still hopping.

He told me that I was too late for dinner, late tea, but that if I were hungry he could send some bread and jam up to the dorms with the van later. I thanked him, said I was fine, and followed him into a door that led down to a basement.

The first thing I ran into once inside a second door at the bottom of the inside steps were stuffed coat racks, piles and rows of boots underneath.

"Take off you jacket and boots. I'll introduce you to Dave. He's the R.A. at St. Ann's, Joachim's." Feeling like a false lamb, I half bounded, half slunk after him past curtained book shelves, a ping-pong table (boxes stuffed underneath), past an upright piano, an old T.V. along the farthest wall. We proceeded up a narrow little flight of stairs to a large, crowded dining area. The first thing I noticed besides all of the cliques of animated folk at most of the tables were the thin metal posts that held up the ceiling in this dining/library area. The kind people use to support sagging basements. Odd, but practical, I thought. A better sign.

The wood tables were simple, almost picnic-like, covered in grey plastic; there were benches under each, end chairs. I felt anxious, expected that, but there was something likable about the place too: a floor so old and worn that I could feel the rising knots in the wood under my stockinged feet. Books were neatly shelved everywhere, library style, complete with Library of Congress call numbers, each section titled: Catholic Saints, Mariology, Christology.

There was a big picture of Tolstoy on the wall at the other end, a librarian's desk, a small card catalog. These guys didn't mess around. And to my immediate left from the top of the basement stairs, a wider set which led to what I was to learn was an upstairs chapel. At the base of those stairs, to the left of them was a display of Ekaterina Fyodorovna Kolyschkine's books.

I had never heard of the woman. Some kind of Catholic Swedenbourgian, Magery Kempe mystic I guessed, judging by the titles of the books: POUSTINIA, KINOSIS. Exotic language for the finer esoteric points of mysticism, no doubt. I leaned over, picked one up, trying not to be obvious in avoiding all the people.

Some of them were quite lively, sitting in groups, but some sat by themselves, too, with little shoe boxes in front of them. They looked to be writing letters. Other people carried trays, empty cups and pitchers out of the room. It was all noisy, controlled. Having just been to college, I just wasn't used to seeing this many alert people in one room, so I didn't know quite what to make of it.

Before I could continue my evasion, actually read any of the material, Patrick came over and introduced me to Ed, the man who ran the work crew. He was a good-sized guy, about my height, but broader, with short hair, lots of energy. He shook my hand, looked right into my eyes, slapped me playfully on the back, said I looked like a man who could use the rigors of farm life.

"Just call me hayseed," I said, trying to get with the program, at least on a surface level.

"Not to worry, James. We'll put some gas in that tank, Praise God."

That stopped me in my tracks. Where on earth did that come from? What did this guy know about my tank anyway? He saw something in me and spoke the truth. That's how I see it now. But back then it irritated me. I liked my privacy, didn't like feeling exposed. I might have even said something smart in reply, given more time, blown the whole gig had it not been for the fact that everybody around me, as if by some unspoken command, rose.

"They've realized," I joked to myself.

It was 10 o'clock, I was to learn. Time to sing "Salve Mater." They all knew it by heart, and once again I was thrown in and left to swim. Should I know this? Was it required Catholic ritual? Finally I just closed my eyes, wondered how the heck I was going to get out of that place.

There was a bustle of activity after the song. Dave, my R.A. man, introduced himself, had a coat, hat, gloves for me to try on as he lead me through a maze of people, through the basement. Outside, dressed, duffel bag and jacket under arm, I was pointed to the brown van, followed some other young men who were obviously headed in the same direction.

All of us shivered in the cold, some jumping up and down, waiting for Dave, who had a few quick errands to run. My coat fit me nicely, an old sailor's, heavy blue, a good, thick flip-up collar and blue knit hat, a tuque, as they called them. I pulled it down past my, by now, freezing ears.

There seemed to be what looked like an enfeebled orchard across from us in the middle of the compound. It was surrounded by an old log-rail fence. A sign post off to the right, like the kind you'd see in a MASH episode, shook slightly in the wind. So many miles to places like Gravelbourg, to Carricou, West Indies, to Flagstaff, Arizona, to Freetown, Liberia, to Paris. (These were, I was to learn, some of their soup kitchens and prayer houses.)

On the far side of the orchard there was another white house, what looked like a bridge, and some ancient gas pumps between that house and the green sheds attached to the main house, which was off to the far right. On each side of the gravel parking lot I was standing in there were other houses, both very small—what I was later to find out were the infirmary and an older men's staff house. Women guests walked across the road I had come in on. I wondered why we had to go to our dorms in a van. Couldn't they find a closer place, especially in this sparsely populated area? Maybe they just want to keep us away from the holy babes.

One guy shivering next to me, sporting a great square Amish or Orthodox beard, was struggling with cold hands to roll a cigarette.

"Welcome to Ice Station Zebra. Colder than a witch's nose. Hi, my name's Mickey." I shook his one hand as he precariously tried to balance his half-rolled cigarette paper in the other, introduced myself, though I was cold and slightly put off by his feminine demeanor. Still, he seemed a likable fellow once I got past that. All for one, that kind of thing. What were we in together on was my question.

There were ten other guys counting Dave who piled into the van, all of whom labored to generate heat as it warmed up. You didn't have enough space to genuinely shiver, so a few of the guys made do. They jostled into each other, shoulder to shoulder to create friction, stamping their feet at the same time just to remind their toes and feet who they belonged to. I got introduced to the five guys in my immediate far back vicinity, but the names came too fast, and I forgot them almost immediately.

"There'll be a quiz in the morning," Mickey said.

I got what I was soon to recognize as the usual volley of questions. Who was I, where was I from, how had I heard about the place? Other splinters of conversation had begun as well, so soon enough my comments were more or less swallowed up as people went back to their own concerns.

I did talk a little bit with a soccer player from New England. Hubert was his name. Told him I was sorry about that. He laughed a little, but seemed strangely silent to me, a taciturn New Hampshirer perhaps? He said he'd come out here to get his life on track. (There was an unwritten rule at The Madonna's Farm. Don't ask people too much about their pasts. But at this time no one had told me about it, so I pried for all I was worth.)

"Why here?" I asked. "Too many drugs, firearms?"

He gave me a pained smile, rubbed his face. "Drugs, yeah. I need a lot of healing. A priest told me about this place. Said it might be a good place to slow down, allow the Lord time to work things out."

"I'm running from the Feds personally. Boot-legging, prostitution, selling illegal crucifixes." I watched for his response. Part of him wanted to laugh, but another part of him felt like he was supposed to be put off. "Na," I said. "Actually I'm converting from the Urdu religion. Goat sacrifice. For the snausages. We worshipped George Washington's eye on the dollar bill."

"Hasn't everybody?" he said. "I just felt too much pressure out there myself, too many demands. People hounding me about which direction I should take with my life. Here I can put my feet out," and he did so.

"A joke. Nice." We both laughed.

We took a quick right after a couple of miles, and by the time we had finished a full circle turn from the main road, we were there. A smallish white house, a porch. The guy who was in the front passenger seat jumped out immediately, took the key off of the ledge just above the door. A silly kind of precaution, really, I thought, considering how far we were away from anyone. Like a person couldn't just break the glass or wouldn't look in that spot first if he were bent on a more mannered version of B & E.

Oh well, I figured, roll with the Catholics.

It was only a matter of minutes before we were all in the kitchen. Guys began brushing their teeth in the sink, washing up out of wide white metal bowls, each taking his personals: a towel, shampoo, toothbrush from his slot behind a curtained partition, each with a combatant's name taped below it. Some guys in another van came in soon after, all of them living down the hill in a more primitive cabin, St. Joachim's, where there were only kerosene lamps and a wood burning stove.

It was very crowded in the kitchen, noisy. In the next room, the first floor bedroom, three guys were sitting at a table, discussing whether it was possible to attain perfection in this life. I was too tired from the travel to try and make anything out of the whole scene, wanted just to take a quick shower, get into my hair-shirt and go to bed.

Dave informed me, however, that showers weren't allowed during the week. Well water conservation. He even went so far as to request that I not flush after urination, at least until the bowl was good and yellow. What if we all had low sugar content, I asked, and what about number two?

"The outhouse down the hill."

My first venture into the unknown dark night of faith, I figured, as I put my out-to-sea coat back on. The green, upright wooden structure seemed sturdy enough, a little hook on the inside. But it was quite cold by then, and I was worried about sitting on the cold plastic seat. Would I stick, have to call for help, many popsicle sticks to pry me loose? But eventualities had been foreseen. There was a winter aid on the wall: a styrofoam doughnut cut-out.

When I finished I took my time returning, looked up at the stars. Never had I seen them so clearly. The milk in the way, the gauze in a clear sky, the whole thing sharp and precise enough for me to wonder if there was anything to this God business. Was there a place so far away that it had no stars, nothing? How could there be an end to the universe; how could there not be? If there was a God, none of these guys seemed to be getting rich off of Him, at least on the surface of things, that seemed clear enough.

Davie directed me upstairs, where I found my bunk among many. They had recently ripped out a partition; I could see the newly sanded and painted strips along the walls and ceiling. Familiar metal posts held the place up. On the far side, Mickey bunked next to me, to my right, away from the stairs. A guy named Ted next to him, by the window. On the other side of the aisle from Ted was a huge bearded guy, Tom, who occupied that first bed. Nick, from Akron, came next, then Daoud, a Palestinian Christian Arab, and Greg, a painter from Minneapolis. Richard from Regina was at the other window end on my side, just across from the stairwell, and Jean-Michele on my immediate left, from Mon-re-al, as he said in disdained English, his bikini red underwear.

Daoud commented that we could be an American basketball team because of our height: Ted, Adam, Nick and myself. Tom, though, seemed slightly offended by that, as he seemed to be by the nickname he had been given. (He did look like the first man.) I thought of Hubert downstairs. Hospital ward.

Nick, however, was a different story. Very expansive, he welcomed the world, me included, heartily. He said we could all be monks on Mt. Athos, at least judging by so many bearded appearances; he didn't want to discriminate against the clean-shaven. Everyone laughed.

Daoud called out in a high voice, "May it be so. Christ is risen!

"Truly," Tom added, perhaps, it seemed to me, because he had learned to do as much. He certainly didn't seem moved by any noticeable enthusiasm when he said it. Struck me as odd. Cultish behavior? "We do want to be ready to greet Him when He comes," he added.

"Speak it, brother," said Jean-Michele.

"You and Rich can throw open your windows," said Ted. "Just in case He comes tonight; stick your feet out to stay alert. Let us know."

Rich smiled—a quiet one.

"I think I'll just keep my candle lit," said Nick with a grin, crawling cozily under his several covers.

"That's okay by me," said Jean-Michele as he pulled out his double eye-patch sleeping mask, put it on. (Everybody seemed to take delight in his wearing this.)

"What are you doing here? That's what I want to know," joked Tom. More laughter.

"Taking a vacation. Now if you don't mind, I would like to get some sleep. Call for me at about 10ish, won't you?"

"Yes, your highness," said Mickey. "Crumpets then, the morning paper?"

"That will do." Someone threw a book in his general direction. Jean-Michele lifted one wing of his eye-patch. "Rabble," he sniffed, amid the last wave of laughter, groans.

Things got quiet quickly—a hard day of work it looked like. And then, some time later, I saw Daoud get up in semidarkness before a little icon of Christ that he had apparently placed on his dresser. He prayed there quietly out of some book for a good fifteen minutes, turning the pages, rocking back and forth slightly as he read. Nick saw me watching him from across the room, winked in my direction.

"You just never know about this place," he whispered, smiling. Then he turned over, fell asleep.

I had said nothing during the whole course of conversation. Wondered how well I would get to know these guys, what they would mean to me. As it turned out, most of them just passed through my life like so many others had before. They each left an impression, favorable mostly, and then were gone. The story of my life, anybody's really, but the story of this place too, in a special sort of way. People came through all the time. Some would stay for a week, some for a month some for a year or two. Those who really liked it found "vocation," stayed for what promised to be the rest of their lives. But for most of us, it was a matter of learning to enjoy the place, the people, and then having to leave it all behind.

3.

Morning came earlier than I would have been comfortable with. Six o'clock. And then the rush again. Dave assigned me a towel rack, a space, and I washed off as best I could. A quick pit job, like the others, a floss in Jean-Michele's case. Some shampooed, everyone combed, brushed. Girls at breakfast, had to be. I liked Jean-Michele right off, a French Canadian who mistrusted everyone that wasn't. "Free Quebec," I'd say when I passed him. He liked that.

I piled, freezing, into the van with him and Nick, waited for the others. I asked what was next as Nick read: cold, ungloved fingers on his Bible.

"You shall see, my crass American friend. Regimentation. It's all designed to keep us from the girls," smoke puffing in front of the fried Frenchman, both of us stamping our feet.

"You mean we don't get to work with the women-folk? I'm againest it, I teail you," I said, feigning spit. "We neaiver do that in Tennessee. Heck, my Aunt Jule, Uncle Bob, they met that way.

Been married fer years. . . . Thaiy're the same person, you know," I said, tucking at him severally under the ribs.

He looked at me as if my head were on backwards, said "Watch out for this one," to Tom, who was just entering the van.

"If Jean Michele doesn't trust you, let me shake your hand," he said with a huge grin.

"Tainted," I said, extended my hand, and soon we were all shuffling over, making room for the late arriving, stamping our cold feet.

Once we were on the road I asked Nick what we would do first. "Not to worry. Just follow the crowd. Someone will always be around to direct you. A service of the place, I think," he said flashing his big Ukrainian smile.

"A nice change from the outside world," added Tom. "We'll load up the van for the farm first, then lauds in the chapel. After that, my favorite, breakfast," (he smiled), "then work. They'll probably send you to the farm. New people usually go there first." I nodded, got the picture, breathed a white sigh. Work. I was agaienst it.

I was going to say something to Nick, but he was back in his Bible again. Everyone was lulled to silence by the sound the bitter cold ground made as it tested the morning tires, as we backed out and onto the main road, the beautiful white countryside opening all up around us, freezing exhaust trailing like a small fugitive flag.

At least four inches had fallen overnight; the trees were caked with luffs of snow, and the clear, cold pale blue early morning sky seemed, itself, frozen, breakable.

When we got to the main compound, the van backed up to the kitchen door. The guys formed a line, and into the vehicle went cold, empty milk containers, a myriad of plastic buckets, wooden shelf beds for bread, two egg baskets, jugs and bottles.

An attractive young aproned woman helped with things on her end. And judging by how cleanly both male and female embraced the new day, the humor that passed between them, I didn't see any strain between the sexes. What had Jean-Michele been talking about?

That finished, Greg, an artist, came over from his place in line, introduced himself.

"Day one, eh? So how do you like the place so far?" he laughed. "Has anyone suggested the priesthood to you yet?" When I said no, he responded, "Just wait. I'm taking bets. We'll keep track. If someone mentions it within three weeks, I win a buck."

"On you like a Woolworth's suit, huh?"

"My mother should be so persistent. Three different people this last week alone." He lead, walking away from the house, into a brisk wind, tears forming, running horizontally on our wind-swept faces. Ice began forming on his beard.

"What's up now?" I asked, clapping my huge deerskin mitts.

"Lauds."

"Does this mean we have to pray. Will people be watching?"

"Yeah, can you believe that? Praying. Next thing you know, they'll be telling us where to work, what we can eat. How did I get here? I don't remember."

Walking between St. Paracletus and the orchard, we found ourselves joining others as we eventually turned right, past some outhouses, garages, a compost heap, shuffling our feet through the newly-fallen snow in the process. And at Greg's pace, we passed a good deal of them, most of whom had smiles, a good word for him.

"Geez, these people actually seem to like you. Have they talked to you yet?"

"They see the collar," he said, smiling grimly.

Soon we came to the chapel. It was beautiful, out in the middle of the woods, evergreens, limited undergrowth on all sides. Made out of huge square logs, coated a rough brown, it was built out of almost as much mortar as wood. Constructed by someone who was a real craftsman, it had a bright golden dome, a Byzantine cross on top: simple, with all the beauty that can come with that.

We opened a wooden door with horizontal fleur-de-lis metal supports, and stepped inside. I was surprised. There were no pews, just a highly polished floor where the younger people knelt in their socks. Older staff members sat on benches that were built into the walls along the back sides, left and right. Up front was a simple Western altar, with cross-slatted gates and a partitioning iconostasis behind it leading to the Byzantine sanctum, a silver dove hanging from a chain above the deeper altar.

Icons of Mary holding a baby Jesus, and Jesus, full grown, his sandal strap unfastened, each hung on one of the partitioning walls. Smaller pictures of the Apostles dutifully hung along side of those. The pictures, icons, like the chapel itself, were executed by someone who knew what she (as it turned out) was doing.

On the left side of the chapel, above a side door was a carved wooden relief of the Infant, in swaddling clothes, with the words underneath: "Lord, give me the heart of a child and the awesome courage to live it out." I was dumbfounded by what I could only call the devotion of all these normal-looking people. Some of the young ones in the middle prostrated themselves in their socks, on forearms, forehead, Jean-Michele included.

Some of the others knelt straight up, some sat crosslegged, hands, palms up, at their sides. What was I doing here, I wondered? Insulting Martians, what they believed in, basically. They didn't deserve this, that much was clear, but I didn't want to go back to where I had been either. I'd just have to be respectful, play things off as best I could until I could figure out a next move. Maybe I'd get turned on to something up here, get wind of a good job down south, an opportunity.

Everyone, I noticed, had taken a book of Psalms and folder of songs from the shelves near the back door. So I retreated and did the same. And sliding down next to Greg, who was among those kneeling straight up, I couldn't help but notice that he was quiet and rapt, his hands folded in front of him. I sighed, closed my eyes, sat there cross-legged, tried to become invisible.

Brought to attention by a tuning pipe, I rose with everyone else, fumbled as they did, with my Psalm book and listened as the singing commenced. Each side of the chapel alternated, sang the basic tones of what must have been the Gregorian chant, call and response. It was extraordinary in its simplicity, took me somewhere else. To feeling, but not to me feeling. I wondered why I had never heard anything like that before in my life. It made me feel like I was waking up on some new morning road, surrounded by a fading mist.

It went on for three Psalms, then we sang a few hymns from the folder. These too, simpler, and yet at times more complicated, riff-wise, than any hymns I'd ever heard before. More haunting notes that moved me to the spiritual reality that held things together, that sang through them.

At least it seemed so to me, for the duration of that song anyway. The schola, as they were called, led the singing. I edged over closer to them. Who were these guys?

Some readings followed, and then, after some silent sitting I wondered, was it time to leave? I couldn't tell right away, grew a little anxious. Some people scurried out of there as if they had somewhere to get to. The kitchen staff perhaps. But most stayed on, informally visiting the icons. People lined up to stand in front of these pictures, touch them with their hands or lean into them bodily, foreheads against the paint. It was odd all right, but quiet and reverent; no one seemed to be putting on a show. No P.R., high hair and fancy t.v. sets for Jesus the winner.

Finally, as the numbers dwindled, I felt safe in going outside, in following the others. There were bushes along the sides of the wide dirt road. I could have slipped away before breakfast, ducked out, hoofed it back and gotten my clothes, been out of there before anybody knew I was gone. I might have, too, had not Tom and Nick caught up to me.

Tom was in a good mood, slapped me on the back. When he laughed, wide, at one of Nick's snow comments, he threw his arms out playfully, as if all of creation had a part in the grand good way of things. Nick, on the other side of me, had by that time, though, moved on to a different subject: Padre Pio and the smell of roses. He had been reading the priest's biography and was into the miracles: the Franciscan standing in the middle of the air during WW II bombing raids, warning away allied planes; all the Confessional wonders, strange ellipses of time, bilocations: how he appeared all over Saint Peter's Square during the beatification of St. Therese, the

Little Flower. I nodded my head when the situation called for it, tried to figure how I could get off the grounds.

The basement was packed by the time we came in. "You should see this place in summer," joked Nick. "Then it's really gets crazy." I hadn't noticed it before, but there were slots behind the coat racks where the staff got their mail, kept books, reminders. There were more library shelves, curtained, to the left of us as well. These were cramped quarters with people all over the place. But no one seemed to mind. Everyone, taking off their boots and coats, gabbing: guests gabbing, staff gabbing, everyone gradually working their way up to the dining room.

By the time I got upstairs, I saw men shuttling in and out of the kitchen with trays in their hands, bowls of steaming porridge or yogurt or honey, all of it homemade. (I would later learn that was one of the men's tasks.)

Most of the tables were full, a priest at the head of each. No escape for me. At the table I chose, the priest was an older fellow with a gray beard, dated glasses, a Father Gene. He was up there, in years and tears, I figured, a busy old goat. Harmless, a safe light and harbor, I hoped, somewhere to duck into the reeds, avoid the holy gab and gunfire. But he was anything but safe. He was the most focused person I'd ever seen in my life; that became clear the more I watched him during the meal.

He was all over what was in front of him, the duty of the moment as I later learned it was called. When he was jamming his bread, that's where he was, listening to someone if they were speaking to him, but his whole consciousness, otherwise, was on the bread.

That may not seem like such a big deal, but how many people really live like that? Most people take great pains to be distracted, or, like my old girlfriend Judy, they become so absorbed in the "spiritual" significance of each act that they can never really unself-consciously live them. They either put their jam on, vaguely aware of what they are doing, or else make the spreading such a vast and obvious prayer that they live, abstracted from themselves, the act. Not this guy. Here was, I see now, real and true humility.

His actions were examples of supreme obedience. It was how he lived his life—doing each little thing well, dying to himself in the moment—because Catherine, a mouth and wound of Christ, preached it. And even if I couldn't recognize back then what was behind all of this, I still had to admit that his apparently selfless attention to things around him was worth a hard look. Not a minute of his life wasted.

He and everyone at the table were all very friendly. They listened as I told them my name, how I had heard of the place. I was a bit tired of the question by this time, however, and decided to make up a new answer whenever anybody asked. This time I chose the life of a house painter.

There was a young woman to my right on the side plank, a man and a woman on the other, and a server to my left. Topics ranged from fasting to liturgical seasons to Father Gene's time spent in the RAF as chaplain during WWII. It was Lent, news to me at this time, so that was the central concern: the desert of the ordinary, the temptation of Christ, spiritual darkness. Occasionally some news about what was going on in the bush would be discussed at tables. Current events, too, came up over the months that I was there, usually with a sense of foreboding. Canadian or American politics. (They would read their own news after dinner on Tuesday night. A holy Brokaw standing and delivering off the page.)

Meals were a crucible for me, especially at the beginning. I was trapped with these people until the bell rang, had to put up with all the lulls in conversation—most of which, I felt sure, were my neurotic fault—everyone near the end of the meal with a toothpick in his or her mouth, in his own silence, other tables laughing. Once I began to loosen up, though, I began to enjoy it, the good humor sometimes approaching rowdiness. That was a ways away at this point though. I was at the beginning just hanging on, feeling the pressure of not belonging, the pressure my presence helped create at each table I joined. Unbearable really. I creaked with it.

The bell to end the meal came mercifully before a breakdown did on that first day, put an end to my woes. The priests led the closing prayer, the prayer for travelers. And after that, surprise of surprises, more confusion. I really had no idea what to do next, where to go as I got up, followed the cattle through the pens. Ed caught me from the side, told me to meet him outside by the basement door. He said he'd be down in a minute.

I waited as I watched people load the van, others scurrying like programmed saints about the compound. When would the other shoe fall I wondered: indoctrination classes, the wired cap? When would they drill the little holes in my neck, insert the rods? And who was getting what out of this whole deal anyway?

No one had even asked me for any money yet, despite the fact that I was eating their food, using their water, not using their plumbing. Only one person, in fact, had even asked me what my last name was. I didn't know what to make of it all. Nobody lives in this kind of poverty, this kind of vulnerability without a reason.

"James, you want to go with Hubert and sand the paths? After you're finished, if there's time, meet me in the basement of Paracletus."

Hubert walked with me to the green sheds next to the main building. There were buckets inside, two big mounds of sand. "This is a pretty easy job. You get to meet some people, figure out your life's work. Pray if you like," he said with a smile. As we filled two buckets of sand each, he continued. "Maybe it would be best if we each took one side. I'll do what needs to be done on the other side of the compound. You can do this side, the island. Just sprinkle enough sand for traction wherever you see a shoveled path."

"Who shoveled?"

"Some staffers came out during breakfast."

At first I suspected that he had chosen the easy portion for himself, but then I figured, na, he'd probably choose the hardest, call it humility. I could go with that. And it did seem like a good job. No one over your shoulder, telling you what to do every minute.

So I grunted assent, steeped in brotherly concern, and headed for the bridge. It had metaphorical implications after all: the next rise, high ground, and besides, it might prove useful, another way out of this joint should I need to book my way some sub-lunar ice-capped night, all the available VCRs in a bag, Christians with their insufferable kindnesses, their leaflets, barking at my heels.

The bridge itself spanned a marshy area, all frozen now, with high grass rising on the left above snow level. To the right, as I made my way across, sprinkling stardust as I went, was the mostly frozen river. An inlet, closer to me, frozen as well, had been shoveled off. It looked like a skating rink.

Once I got across, I noticed a little cabin to the right. It looked out over the Madawaska. A nice spot. An engraved relief in wood over the door, quoted St. Francis: "God asked me to be a fool the likes of which the world has never seen." Must be the big cheese's cabin. (I found out later I was right. Catherine's.) I was impressed. It wasn't unduly large or luxurious. And I didn't see any outdoor signs of a heater or gas line. Maybe she kept all the gleanings in a Swiss bank account? But I had heard she was a pretty old bird; what was she waiting for, a nice young man to give it all to?

Snow was piled high along the maze of newly shoveled paths on that "island," paths that ran around and between other cabins, to water pumps, to the chapel. At one of the cabins I ran into a very old woman named Yvonne. She had a thick Belgian accent and was what I would later learn was called a Poustinikki, a hermit of sorts. Thin oldish skin, blue veins, limpid eyes, curly gray hair, she was dressed in an opened coat that first time I saw her which she had wrapped around herself on her porch. She was trying to get a squirrel to come for a pine cone she had in her hand. Smiling when she saw me, she eagerly enlisted my help in finding her more of them. I liked the idea, could put the sand bucket down for awhile.

There was an unhurried quality to her that, early on, made me think that what she really needed was some gainful employment, a sense of direction. But the trace of stress in her old facial lines, her calm blue eyes, her thick accent and movement gave me pause. I began to sense some of the peace she was living in.

And in a little while, partly because of her, perhaps, I stood in the middle of spacious sunlight, a ridiculous new joy: her bucket in hand, next to a painted green water pump, the cones I had gathered inside. I was able to watch the channel of blue river move from where I stood, its bright pace between the ice, under the clearest bluest sky I had even seen, the smell of evergreens scrubbing up the breezes.

I wanted that job for the rest of my life. (Could I get that? Was this God thing real?)

My last stop on the island was the chapel. Needing a break, I decided to pop in and take another look around inside. To my surprise, there were a few people still at prayer. One older guy was sitting cross-legged in front of the icon of Christ, and an old woman, along the back, on one of the wall benches, sat looking out a cold, opened window.

As I proceeded with the utmost deliberation, I spotted Hubert corning up the other way on the path, furiously spreading his sand.

"In a bit of a rush, aren't we?" I asked, pausing to breathe in the scent of pine.

"Duty of the moment."

"Whose moment?" He smiled, said perhaps I was right. Maybe he did put too much into things, trying to meet a legalized standard. A subtle form of pride. (Of course, I hadn't meant any such thing. My comment was more one of general suspicion, paranoia even.) I found him funny. "What do you expect to get out of all this anyway?" I asked as I was struck by his desire to please.

"Wow, that's good," he said. Again attributing profound undertones to my grouse. Then he gathered himself, said we needed to go to Paracletus, find Dave.

"Maybe we could split and get a beer or a jay, say we lost our buckets. Broke our crowns or something. The beer came tumbling after. Any stills, Canadian rednecks around here? Ah miss my shotgun, girl cousins."

"At 10:30? Pretty hard core, my friend."

"Call it a gift."

I had crossed the line. I could see that the moment I spoke, but screw it, I thought to myself. I was actually sweating out there!

Dave was down in the basement with some older guy named Tom, both with their shiny crosses hanging from their necks. Only some of the people here had these, the staff members. The basement was, not surprisingly, extremely ordered. The two of them were hard at it, sorting used screws, unbending nails. Not what I had hoped for: my ideas of communal farming ran more toward large doses of Moses David: freely dispensed drugs, random sex, decadence disguised as utopia.

Life, where was thy sting?

But here was where I was. Besides, there was something kind of admirable, basically good, unassuming about these folks. They were there for you; I couldn't deny that. A kind of surreptitious, subterranean hospitality. They offered you a place at their fireside, a chance for you to work with them in their lives. Why would anyone would put himself at this kind of risk I couldn't say. Who knew what kind of pot-pushing degenerate might come through the door?

Before Dave could get us onto anything new, the bell rang for tea. And soon guys were piling into the basement, washing their hands, combing their hair. Six or seven of them. A staff guy I hadn't met yet introduced himself to me. Don. Shook my hand. Clear blue eyes—the open face of a man used to working with his hands, finding what he needed there. He made me nervous, so I ducked out toward the out houses as quickly as possible.

Everyone in the compound (similar goings-on were taking place at the farm) gathered in the dining room for bread and water at this time. No jam, honey, tea, or milk was offered. It was Lent, and abstinence was in order. People stood around or sat in groups, talked. Don saw me looking lost there, I guess, lingering around Catherine's books, came over.

"Do you know the Bee's work?"

"The Bee," I asked?

"Yes Catherine. She's our foundress."

"No. I should, I know. But I've been caught up in the academic life.

You know how it is. Not much time for spiritual reading. Why is she called the Bee?" I couldn't feel anything to grab onto with this guy—no sense of what mattered to him, or how to get there.

He was a blank, with a friendly face. (It was like I was on stage, and my straight man was wearing a mask.) What could I play off of? How could I go along with things if there was no direction given? It made me feel naked, and I wasn't keen on sharing my boils.

Was his an assumed pose I wondered? Other staff workers turned out to be much the same. They'd talk to you, about your life, about spirituality, but never about themselves. (Most of them anyway. Some whom I got a chance to work with for a whole day would open up, and they were real enough.) Maybe this guy was just doing his spiritual job, all the while protecting himself from people who came and went with such regularity. It must be tough, I thought, but still, I had myself to protect as well. I wasn't sure how long I wanted to stay at this place, but I did know that I wanted to be the one to call my own shots.

"A little boy in Harlem, at Friendship house gave her the name. Said she had all the honey. It just stuck after that."

"No pun intended," I said. He smiled. "She worked in Harlem? No kidding, I bet you couldn't do that today?" Keep talking, I thought. Keep smiling.

"Oh no. Actually we have a prayer house there. The Bishop asked us to come. A few people set up shop, pray for the city, offer retreats. I spent three years in Whitehorse doing just that. God does great things in little houses." He smiled.

"Well it seems like he's doing a large work in this large one as well." I was desperate, trying to keep things on an acceptable spiritual level, trying for happy talk, hoping to slip away before I shriveled.

Just then two women came over, Suzanne and Moccasin. Don introduced us, then receded, slapping me on the back, leaving his hand on the area between my neck and shoulder for a moment, giving it a final squeeze.

"She's something," said Suzanne, pointing to the Bee's picture on the back of one of her books. "Bigger than life, don't you think? It takes a lot of courage to live like that." She looked with awe at the picture.

She was an attractive woman, Suzanne, with a bright multicolored scarf around her hair which she kept pulling down at the sides, as if to reinforce her own sense of resolve. Her accent was Charleston, WV, I learned, as they introduced themselves. She had the aura of someone who had been a success in the outside world, was very charming, went out to greet you as an impressive woman does, with the back of the hand presented first.

She had a fine, unfettered smile. Without any obvious pretension. Her open, intelligent beaming face let you know that you were important to her just now, that she anticipated a good interaction. (An expression of her own healthy ego, no doubt as well.) But, still, nice, generous.

And looks. Her cheekbones, skin, perfect lightly pursed lips, light blue eyes. She had been a beauty queen in another life—a Miss Cherry Blossom Festival—I was to later learn. Heal, I said to myself.

"I suppose you're right," I said. "One of the special ones."

"I like her little book on Apostolic Farming," said Moccasin. "That's the way I'd like to go. Live on a farm, raise some pumpkins, both kinds." Suzanne smiled. It was obvious that they had talked about that possibility: family and farming, in some detail.

She was her own bag of seeds: Moccasin. Small, a little hippyish with long frizzed hair, glasses, she had laughing gray eyes, wore loose-fitting clothes, even for that place. She had the slightest little bounce to her walk. You could see how much she loved life in the slightly coy, swirling flip she often gave to her hair, twirling a bit with it. It was an action designed for her benefit as much as anyone else's. She delighted in being able to carry on in such a "female" sort of way, apparently, found it humorous, perhaps, that no one had ever called her on it.

You had to like her. And if she were more quiet, unassuming on some level than Suzanne, less strikingly attractive, she did have a real charm, ease that were all her own. She was easy to get close to I would discover, with her penchant for tea and back-to-the-earth talk, spoke four languages.

"A harmonica and banjo on the porch," I countered. "A little herb in the garden." By the shocked look on Moccasin's face, I could tell that I'd done it again. "Just kidding, just kidding," I quickly a added. "It's a joke." There was a moment of silence.

"It sounds nice to me," said Suzanne, who had missed the reference, looking over to her friend. "God's will be done."

Moccasin smiled. "So, where are you from?" she asked me.

The bell rang soon enough and it was back to work. Hubert and I followed Dave back into Paracletus' basement. He helped us find a few good axes, no easy task as many of them had been damaged by blows just under the metal head. "Swinging too furiously," Dave said. He sent us beyond the orchard, to the wood stacks behind the garages.

Curious, nosey as ever, I asked Hubert what was in the buildings; and, surprisingly, he took the time to show me. (Maybe he was looking forward to chopping as much as I was.) Stacks and stacks of boxes. What were all these for I wondered?

"Clothes to be sorted, for the poor," he said. "Stick around for the weather to break, and you might get to help."

"Maybe I will," I said.

The wood split easily in the cold weather. We tossed the pieces over near the piled stacks until we felt like setting the axes down; then we'd go over and complete the task. Hubert stayed pretty much within himself, so I was free to scheme. How could I blow this pop stand? Where would I go? Though my questions now had the ring, even to me, of concerns that were no longer pressing. I was, although I didn't recognize it at the time, searching for a new orientation, an outlook that would justify my staying there for awhile. I could handle this Lent stuff. The women were nice. There was a peaceful feel to the place.

It wasn't like I had anything to get back to.

4.

Before we knew it, the noon bell rang and it was Paracletus again. To lunch, and after, to hear Catherine talk about God. She was a large woman, of peasant stock it looked like in her loose-fitting cream-colored shift. In her eighties, though one didn't notice that so much when she spoke. Her language was, at times, a little archaic, but it came to us unhurried, with the cumulative power of one who had experienced. Everyone was rapt, at least for the length of his or her respective attention span; you could see it throughout the dining room. Some people working toothpicks, first on one side, then the other. Thumb and forefinger never leaving the wood. Others would lean against the metal posts, feet outstretched on the bench if no one else were there. Some, near the end of her talk though, would drift, their heads buried deeply in their hands. They would lean too far, or an elbow would slide off a knee. The head would drop, surprise them. They'd look around, shocked. Occasionally we'd even hear a brief snore.

I was pretty skeptical that first time, but decided to listen anyway. It was the least I could do for the asylum they'd provided, the food. Besides, she'd apparently lived a full life, and all these folk thought enough about what she had learned to line up and listen, so maybe I might catch a nugget or something.

It seemed an odd joint, hospitality aside. There was no money being made. No sex. No reward, at least of a tangible nature. So why did they all come, really? They seemed, right from the beginning, to be the sanest people I had ever met, and yet here they were, devoted to what? Being peasants? Where was the prize in that?

". . . Christ is in the faces of the poor. We have all heard that before. We hear the sermons everyday in the chapel, exhorting us to give a cup of water to the thirsty, and we are sure we would, too, if we were in the middle of things, in Regina (laughter) or one of the other soup kitchens; if it weren't for our daily, sometimes hum-drum routines: making bread or chopping wood, trying to be nice to someone who, if the truth be known, is not such a pleasant individual." (More laughter.)

She smiled for a moment, continued. "We can even picture it: a beaten man, the Samaritan, along the side of the crossroads in downtown Toronto. We would stop and help him to a hospitality house, right in the middle of all the pedestrian traffic, the heart of Christ moving in us. We would struggle with this poor man, with his weight, his smell; we would help him to his feet.

"And some of us, indeed, would; but how many of us would think like a sociologist, the social register first, staff included? What good would my picking him up do; what good would my giving him food do? Would that teach him how to work or would it reinforce his dependent habits? Maybe in many cases true charity lies in the other direction? Maybe it would be just pride on my part, picking up this man. Pride in every direction. I already have responsibilities after all, duties-of-the-moment that come with that. It would be foolish to expect me to make a halfway house of my home, to ask me to literally pick up every tattered beggar I see.

"FOLD THE WINGS OF YOUR INTELLECT, YOU FOLLOWERS OF CHRIST. . . . LISTEN TO THE SPIRIT. . . . HE WILL LEAD YOU. Become poorer because you are beggars. Be one with them because you are one of them, less than they if the truth be known. You who have been shown much, what have you done? You are the ones being picked up, not them. You are the ones being fed. They are feeding you. If you can't see that, you will lie in your ditch for a long time. Good Samaritans come in all kinds of clothes.

"Reach for the ragged man, crucified on the street, spreading sand, chopping wood. He will feed you. He is what you can do, what you can repay. He is Christ, the one who has no place to lay His head.

"We are not poor enough. That is our problem. I look around here and all I see are rich people in borrowed clothes. People who want meat at meals, people who want insulation in their houses, salt on their tables. . . . Go back to work . . . Go. . . . You disgust me. There is too much distance between you and that poor man, between you and Christ. You value respectability," she said raising her cane. "Take it then, into the fields, to the bread ovens, see how far it will get you." She turned her face.

There was quiet, some rustling. Finally a few people began to meekly get up, start to go to work. Then more. She stopped them before the first got to the door.

"Stop, sit down. . . . How can you reach the heights unless you realize that you are at the bottom? . . ." she asked quietly. And after a long pause, "Let me tell you a story. . . . Once, many years ago, Dorothy Day invited me to come to New York to visit her. . . . A prostitute, late in the night, came after me. . . . There was no place to put her. . . . Where would she sleep? . . . Dorothy did not hesitate. She would sleep between us, on the only bed available. . . .

"Having been a nurse, I wondered if this was such a good idea. The thought of disease, t.b., venereal infection crossed my mind. . . . Dorothy realized my apprehension, looked at me calmly, said, 'Catherine, this is the face of Christ.'" You could have heard a pin drop.

"It's like they say. If you have anything to lose," she said, pounding the table, speaking loudly, "you must lose it. I had to lose Russia, Harlem, Toronto, respectability. I was called a Communist because I was from Russia and valued poverty. When we came up here to this little farm in 1947 because the Bishop asked me to, there was nothing but one broken down old house. So you know what we did? We planted an apple orchard. God would, unbeknownst to us, use us as He always had, in whatever way He chose. That was all we wanted. Nothing for us. Don't you see? Nothing for you. There is nothing for you. If it doesn't hurt you, it's not love. If part of you resists, there is still sin in you. I repeat: it's not about you, your feelings, your ideas. It's about Him, others. Loving them in Him, in your nothingness, which is Him also. It's about losing who you think you are so that you might become who you were made to be.

"It was God again, in 1947, writing straight with crooked lines. I would be a poustinikki for while, until my village came. Until you all came. People I never asked for. Like in Russia. Russia, people! Every hamlet with a church in the center, a hermit under thatched roof on the outskirts, his door always open. I remember my mother taking me, a child of three, a baroness and her daughter, to visit the bearded ones, the staritzes. And as we made pilgrimages from shrine to shrine, monastery to monastery, a rich woman on foot, walking on good Russian sandals, I wondered what it all meant.

"In the night sometimes my heart longs for that mystery, for those days again, for the Russia of my youth. When Christ was at the center of every town, every community." She stopped here, sunk heavily, unself-consciously, in her backless chair, and I got a sense that she was somehow bearing the weight of our foolish communities. She buried her head in her hands, (her grey hair was pulled up on top of her head, braided, bobbie-pinned) eventually rose up out of that.

"Baaah! What do you have today? Communities like Toronto where neighbors don't even know each other. And television. A pop therapist on every corner. People running in circles, trying to avoid the poor man from Nazareth. How fast do you have to run when you are going nowhere to begin with?" She liked that one, twinkled a bit. "Now go, go to work. And work hard. And love yourselves, people, as you love others. That is what you have to give. If you succeed at the little things, smaller ones will follow." She smiled.

I liked her. She was rude, didn't care for what anybody said, thought of her. She didn't bow to anybody, or maybe to everybody. In any case, I felt drawn. She asked for so much, but that was a given for this crowd. What else was worth it, I guessed? Could you follow, she asked? Did you have enough guts to do it?

This was unsure ground, a far cry from my college days: Sunday mornings coming down, the Calvinist hair-hat, pompadour Gospel hour (and that was just the men). I'd sit with my roommates; we'd switch back and forth between those staged amens and big-time rassling body slams in the common room. They seemed of a piece in some way. Pure Americana: the complete victory of style over substance: the yea, the crowd, the cathartic heal and physical pay-off. Everything we wanted out of life, at half the price.

This case seemed different, though. Here was this ornery old bird, somehow peasant and aristocrat at the same time with her simple manner, her high, romantic tone, pointing out to me just how shallow I was. (The nerve!) What could I say?

Maybe it was time to move up. Maybe this poor dead man was calling me? (Though I didn't hear His voice.) And as I drifted back through the steps that immediately proceeded my coming here, searching for clues of grace, my mind, for some reason, flashed farther back, to my Aunt Amelia in Denver. I started remembering her saying all those prayer beads years ago, working her way around the house with that cane, doing her dishes, talking to me, a little boy sitting in a high green chair next to the sink.

I realized then, for the first time, that I had been holding her sickness against her. How childish. She was a good woman, was there for me until she could barely stand, though I didn't notice much of what I registered when I was a kid. I was too busy sulking. I wondered how she was doing, decided to write to her again. But I was interrupted from my reverie by that little bell. Lunch was over.

It angered me, and I decided that somebody ought to lift that sucker. Unfortunately, there was a whole collection of them under the photos behind Catherine's backless perch as I passed her table—she was talking to a female guest. There were pictures of her with Cardinals; an old Pope; with John Howard Griffin, author of BLACK LIKE ME; (her head on his chest) one with her recently deceased husband; one with, I was to learn, Thomas Merton. She'd been around for a long time.

How come I had never heard of her? Was Morley Safer neglecting his duties on 60 MINUTES or what?

I felt like one of the herd again, made moo sounds, garnered a few smiles as I drifted with the mass of people, all of us heading down the stairs. Maybe I'd go to the farm that afternoon, I thought. That might be interesting. But Jean-Michele cut me off.

"Hey, grizzled American, don't you know it's half-day today? What are we up to?" I must have looked puzzled. "Didn't anyone tell you? We have the rest of the day relatively free, until vespers. Are you going to get that coat? . . . Hello," he said, knocking as if on my head. "Is anybody in there?"

"Easy," I half-snarled, then recovered. "Where do I go again to get the coat?"

He looked at me quizzically: "St. Joseph's Center. Come on, I'll walk you up. I want to stop at the restaurant, get some real food," he said, secretively. "Are you interested?" I nodded, so we headed up the road. About half way up we were passed on the other side by two women. "Josie and Clare," he said immediately, yelling a friendly hello. They responded in kind, but neither he nor they made any attempt to cross the street and talk. Very un-Jean-Michele-like it seemed to me. He responded to my query: "Not allowed. We would need a chaperone. Can you believe that? They're afraid of scandal among the locals. Tea's about the only time, though it's not uncommon for a staff member to come over and join your table if you're having fun." The girls turned up the road to the left.

"They have no rutting festivals in the spring then; we don't get to wear horns, paint our faces, do goat dances?"

"Well you can. I think there's a place over there in the woods. But they won't; they're celibate."

"Ouu. . . . Well, I guess, when in Rome. It's an odd world all the way around, don't you think?"

"Here anyway."

St. Joseph's Center, the rural apostolate, was your basic large-scale garage sale. Everything from children's books to old work boots. Staff members ran the place, Janine and Mary Kay. More cars were parked around there than I thought in the vicinity. The lot was filled; there were cars lining the grass on both sides of the lesser road, creating a limited corridor to drive through. The locals had descended with a vengeance.

But things ran smoothly. There was order, if not space. Shoes divided by type, coats by size, color. We even got a cup of orange pecot tea. Donated.

I find it interesting, now that I look back, how well this community lived out Catherine's words: they got along quite well with their neighbors. In order to hit the headlines, get noticed, you've got to get them in a huff, be paranoid and gun-toting. Morley wouldn't be interested in this. It made too much sense.

I found a good coat, a hat, gloves, all for three funny dollars, a few of them thin, questionable Canadian courters. Left my borrowed clothes. I wanted to mill about some, but Jean-Michele was anxious for faster food. And he wasn't alone; before the door finished ringing its bell at the restaurant, we were greeted by a hail of hellos. Tom and Nick were already at table and invited us over, several female guests at a different table. Our two mates were nursing strawberry milkshakes, said they had skipped lunch for this opportunity.

Jean-Michele said he was giving up Lent for Lent, the ultimate sacrifice, but ordered only fries with his shake. I went the whole nine yards, ordered two cheeseburgers, fries, a big coke.

"It's Wednesday and you're ordering meat?" Nick asked.

"I'm not into Lent," I replied, figuring that if I wasn't among friends, at least I wasn't among enemies. Jean-Michele laughed, and the others just looked at each other, Tom's mouth falling open.

"I'm afraid I'm not totally used to all of that good farm food yet. I guess I need some sugar," said Tom, feeling a little guilty.

"Well, there is always Confession," joked Jean-Michele.

"Skipping lunch makes it even, don't you think?" asked Nick. "This adds a little mid-week spice for me. . . . Just this once. Besides, we don't want to get legalistic about it, do we?" an engaging smile spread across Nick's Greek face.

The waitress brought our drinks, smiling, asked Tom and Nick if they needed anything else. Jean-Michele and I just looked at each other.

"Well frankly, I could use a little female companionship," said Jean-Michele after she left.

"I don't know if I agree. This is a place for serious interior work. If the Lord has someone in mind for you, you'll meet her," Tom said.

"Jean-Michele has a vocation," joked Nick. Everyone laughed.

"I suppose that's true. Though let's do a thorough search before we jump into anything, eh?" smiled Jean-Michele.

"So James, you're from Cleveland?" Nick asked.

"My last stop," I said. "So why are you so up all the time, anyway, if I can ask? I've never seen anybody smile that much who wasn't up to something." I smiled, tried to gain some spiritual ground, didn't want to come off like the complete pagan I was.

"Joy of the Lord. Gratitude. I don't want to take the credit for anything," he said, smiling. "God is so good. I went through most of my life without even realizing how much is possible. Joy. It's the fruit of the Spirit." Apparently he didn't want to sound too pious, so he took pains to modulate his tone. "Watch it. . . . I might just start dancing on the table."

"Please, not that Charismatic stuff again," said Jean-Michele.

"Well, I'd like to hear more about it," Tom said, as the man from Mon-re-al started lolling his tongue around, making noises like Linda Blair in the EXORCIST. Nick remained relatively discreet.

"Father Beltin says they're going to do a Life in the Spirit some time this spring. So the opportunity might come up."

"No thanks," Jean-Michele concluded.

The volleys continued. Finally, though, after we'd all had our fill of water and coke, we headed back. I walked alone, behind in the cold, needed to think about what Nick had said. He seemed like he had his head on straight. So why was he talking about gratitude? I didn't see that there was so much to be grateful for: war, famine, the violence inside all of us, inside of God.

There was time before vespers when I got back, so I ambled around in the basement, looking for something to do. The ping-pong table was being used; someone was on the piano, another person accompanying on guitar. It was pleasant to lean against a bookshelf, listen for while, but I got restless, went outside. I hadn't seen the front of the house yet, so I highstepped my way through the snow, around to my left after I came up from the basement. A little path led me past a very unusual statue of Mother Mary. It was like she was flying: bluish, coppery, her veil blown back, her arms outstretched. As if she were coldly, mysteriously coming for each devotee.

There was a nice view out front, lawn chairs covered with snow, a nice view of the Madawaska. It was still very cold. You could hear the occasional loud crack of ice some mornings, still see smoke out over the water, the air colder than the river. It couldn't have been anymore than five degrees out there, a cold snap someone at lunch had said.

It was at this point that I heard people carrying on over to the left, so I followed the echoing sounds to the inlet on the river-side of the bridge. Guests and staff had lined up barrels on either side of the shoveled rink. Two per side, the inside space being the goal area. Contestants were armed with brooms so old that they were without yellow straw below the sewn threads. It was hockey on ice, played in boots, no skates. It looked like great fun, what with the high banks of snow serving as boards.

The pace was civil; no one got blasted, though some did meet the weather conditions face-to-face. I stood on the sidelines, enjoyed the futility of the game. Daoud noticed me first, waved me over enthusiastically, said their side needed all the help they could get. I had never been one for sport up until this time; it had always seemed too fascist a deal: win one for the Gripper. But this was big fun because everyone was inept out there. Everybody looked ridiculous. If your feet didn't trip you up, a housemate would.

I liked the concept. So I played, would try to run, my cartoon feet going much faster than I could. I couldn't control direction, couldn't stop; people comically took to saying hello and good-bye whenever anybody slid by, out of control, everyone getting good and sweaty with the wasted effort.

Vespers came too soon. I wanted to keep on playing, lay there on a bank, my cherry cheeks, wet and cold, my hot breath, heavy breathing. But there was such cheer in the winding-down that I happily went with the flow, felt my face and feet burn as I warmed up in the chapel.

There was a chalice on a small back table this time. People put hosts in as they entered. And once again, that music: simple, where the heart is, rising to God's low, deep own, if He was and had one. I was moved by the simple faith of these people. They weren't perfect, I knew that. I'd already seen some of their flaws. But they were honestly confronting their condition, without the frills, at least what they assessed it to be. That was admirable. And they were prospering personally, if not financially, in doing so.

Of course, if all of this did anyone any good out in the real world was another question. Maybe they figured that we, the few, the proud, could take some of it back, bring about the beginnings of change. Convenient, then, this cold oasis? Maybe. But it wasn't easy; they had to show up everyday, not collect their pay.

Any reservations I had were swallowed up in the Mass that followed, at least for a time. I had always seen ritual as a hollow hope, if the only one some people had. That was pale recommendation enough for me, in a world that offered little otherwise. Whatever got one through the night. But I was amazed at this service.

The priest, a Father Wold, spoke from another place: unashamed, holy it seemed, patient in being there. When he said, "Let us pray," he meant it, would move back into a profound silence he obviously spent a great deal of time in, his whole presence somehow filled with light. Slow, illumined, he'd rock back and forth behind the altar; and when he gave his sermon, he spoke from a mutual, simple place, common to all of them. All of them at home in what he called "the desert of the ordinary."

It was by me. All this gratitude in picking up a needle, in the splitting of logs. I didn't get it. The One who becomes more, he said, as we become less. None of them had suffered from the transition, though, that much was clear.

I didn't know what to think. And then when he raised the Host, he left us for awhile. I don't know how else to put it. The simple bright peace on his face said enough, him vacationing, just he and the Stone Other. I tried to blend in with those seated as people formed two lines to go up, get fueled. Catherine appeared from the left. I hadn't even noticed her there though she was wearing a bright stocky red dress with colorful beaded embroidery about the neck.

There was something special about her, I couldn't deny it. A bright presence, an aura of real power, spiritual power. I actually felt repelled by its force as she passed in front of me on her way up to Communion.

I was going to join in the procession, fake my way through, just to make it appear as if I belonged, but that didn't seem right after seeing her there. This was serious business to these folks. I didn't want to walk on that. I also knew that in not doing so I would mark myself as one who needed counsel. Well, that had never been a secret I figured, so no big deal there.

Noh-dinner was bread and tea. Lent again. I wondered how long this would go on. Hand me my whip, the discipline, like they talked about at the dorm: "Thank You, Lord. May I have another!" What was the point of all this. I wondered, nibbling on my bread? Would this make them holy or remind them that they were not? Why not at least eat when considering the possibilities?

Afterwards there was the chore known as "vegetables" in the basement below the kitchen. All the men guests would stand around pails of water and peel, shave, cut anything plant-like that needed to be so dealt with. There was always much conviviality. Sex was never discussed; sports, hardly ever. But there was no shortage of conversation. Papal encyclicals, politics around the world, personal playful slurs, banter on the subject of vocation. (Greg wincing.)

Visiting priests pitched right in with the rest of us, someone in the kitchen making suggestions whenever needed. They were followed without fuss. People, busy in relative harmony: self-seeking, taking, at least from all appearances, second place. I wondered what I would have to do to jump into the middle of all of this, become part of it, instead of just sitting back on the periphery like I had always done. I could become a Catholic, like Aunt Amelia, take Communion. I didn't know yet, but decided to just keep saying the right things, listen hard; I could learn from these people.

Things were changing for me.

It was as clear as those bright yellow buckets. I would rather be like them than like me. There was a light there, purpose, and, even if I didn't see it at the time, I was beginning to turn, gratefully, to meet that Light.

Evenings were a time for playing backgammon, reading, visiting, or going to classes when they had them. Sometimes there would be staff meetings, at other times the "Bee" would meet with the working guests in a big room upstairs, answer questions, relay her past. It was a pleasant time all in all, evenings, though you couldn't call them a break from the day. There was none of that, except for the times when a visiting priest would pile in with us in one of the guest's cars, the occasional Wednesday evening, hotfoot it over to Ottawa or the next town for a beer, some 8-ball.

On one of my first evenings, I spent some time with Clare, a beautiful mostly French-speaking little tomato from Quebec. The bluest eyes, deep cut lines between cheeks and mouth, smooth skin. She was practicing her English on me, and I was getting along rather well with my French until Dave came up, asked me into the other, front Madawaska room.

Nice place: windows, books, magazine racks. He said, as we sat alone at the long table in there, that he was concerned about the drug thing. Had I been taking them before I came up? How long was I off them, was that the case? They had had bad experiences in the past and needed to be cautious. I was as forthright as I dared to be, with respect, because I was just beginning to like the place and didn't want to leave. I told him about Mingo, my discomfort with my job, my resignation. About how I moved up to Cleveland, and with the help of grace, started grad school in literature. And the dope, just a few harmless tokes with fellow students at a party one night. I told him it gave me a headache, that I didn't inhale, had to go and sit in a closet until I came down. An unpleasant evening all the way around. I told him that there was no cause for worry, that everything was okay. God had taken me through all of that. I wanted to stay.

He sat back, rubbed his chin. After a very pregnant pause, we prayed together. When he came back, he said he'd be willing to let it go, reluctantly. But if I had any problems with my past, I should seek him out or a priest or the staff doctor.

Then he switched gears, asked me who I liked poetrywise. Hopkins, Dante, definitely. Did I like Alice Meynell, Peguy, Lionel

Johnson, Chesterton, "The Hound of Heaven," and what about fiction: Mauriac, Bernanos, Waugh, Greene? I said I'd put them on my list, tried to edge away. But before I could do so, he mentioned that I might consider picking out a priest as a spiritual director, a guide.

Jean Michele greeted me as I came out. "The third degree, eh?"

"Yeah, they's askin about my relatives in Tennessee."

Then the bell rang and the nightly song ensued. I actually picked up a few words, eyes still closed. When we got back to the dorm, though, I made it a point not to speak to anyone, set my jaw and went right to bed.

5.

As we rolled toward Easter, I finally got to spend a long stretch of consecutive days on the farm. Janine, a different one, drove the van out after loading. It was about five miles to St. Benedict's Acres. On the way out the first day, we slowed down to salute one of the visiting priests who was taking a brisk hike from his residence at Carmel Hill—it was out even further in the boonies—to the Main House. For health reasons. After we passed him, someone mentioned his life in Eastern Europe under the Communists before he had been smuggled out: prison, torture, starvation.

Whiner.

This extremely short fellow came out of the back door of the farmhouse to greet us, tuque in his hand, as we got out of the van. He was relatively young, monastic looking with his naturally balding head, short hair, ready smile. Richard was his name.

And before I could voice a preference—one never did—I was out there chopping wood again in what felt like fine, brisk zero degree weather. Surprisingly enough, the conditions were manageable, at least once you'd figured out how to cope. Jumping up and down on my toes until I could feel them again always worked for me. Once I gotten that far, I'd be good for the whole morning. But that having been accomplished, I still had to deal with the wood pile thing again. The constant repetition of the place was getting to me.

I got set up between an outhouse and an aluminum corrugated half-moon shaped building which was filled with horse harnesses, tools, all the merciless physical details of farm life. And though I tried to amuse myself by measuring the relative effectiveness of my strokes, how hard a swing it would take to split what sized log, the whole thing bored me to frozen tears. There was no getting around it: the "ordinary" could be staggeringly boring. So, resourceless, I'd stop, sit down on the logs, see how far I could spit in the snow, look out over the horizon, clap my mitts and listen for the echo.

The hills across the way offered some consolation. They looked frosted, the trees, like earthen bristles, covered as they were with snow. But even that didn't last. Chop, chop, stack, stack, take this monkey off my back. Try as I might, I couldn't do much to keep my mind off of my predicament. (I even tried making angels in the snow.) What kind of life was this anyway, I wondered, out chopping wood with no visible means of support except these puppet wires, and me, 24 years old, strong and lame as I could be? If God was so real, why couldn't He at least be interesting? Give me a life?

Part of me wanted to bury the ax in corrugated tin, take off through the trees, find some wolves, bear grease, night fires. I could learn to grunt on all fours, smear the entrails of animals into a large circle. At least that would be living. Druid and stupid, but living. Not this barter-my-time-for bread-and-routine routine.

But before I got farther into my grouse, I was interrupted by singing. It started from the upstairs of the little farmhouse. About sixty yards away. Farmers praying. And it came to me. This was it for these guys. There would be no Hollywood nights at a later date, no short tight skirts, Bentleys. And it became clear, too, that they had chosen the harder part. This wasn't an escape from the outside for them, but a more difficult way. What could you run away from in here after all? You couldn't hide beneath your latest jag. There were no jags to be had. Here you had to get up the next morning and do the same damned thing you did the morning before for years at a time or until someone gave you a different, impossibly ordinary job. It would have driven me up the complete wall. And yet there they were, singing through it. Happier than clams, or at least they seemed to be, happier than anybody I had ever known. That much was sure.

Father Beltin talked about service, freedom, the God of the ordinary at lunch.

"We are called to use every minute to grow during the hard days; we are called to allow ourselves to be cracked open by Love . . .

"And what will we be left with at the end of our days? A little gratitude, a little dross . . .

"This is where true joy is, in the difficulties. . . .

"And then we will look around one day, without even having ever thought about it, and we will be holy. We will be friends of God!

"Like Catherine says, 'He tells us, "Come up higher."' Love, love, love, never counting the cost. Move in that love if you feel it or not. Move in Nazareth, in the ordinary. . . . This is our part."

When I went back to work, I thought about what I had caught of the teaching. Holiness. Is that what all of this was about? What about my writing deal? What about Buffy, my home in Malibu? All jags . . . to prove I was living. . . . Yes, I had to be honest. . . . That's all those things were. And I knew too that I didn't want to spend the rest of my life in trying to get them: the kudos, the perfect looking female appendage.

We moved through Lent, me spending more and more time at the farm. With another David, a staff member, I helped make yogurt and cheese. At other times I held sheep by the scruff of the neck as someone delivered a clean hole into the forehead. We hung 'em high, upside down as the guts flopped, horribly into Whitman's pail. Then we mule-skinned the lambs, punching fists between skin and muscle pulling down the pelts like the unwanted portions of our lives.

I'd go up to the cross at the top of the hill sometimes during tea, for the solitude it afforded. Was the aloneness I felt like Christ's I wondered? Maybe to some degree. A large part of mine, though, was, more honestly, for a woman, for some concurrent action. It was too tough a sledding, I decided, this place. There was no comforting insanity. No chance to run gleefully through the forest once in awhile, naked, ram my head against a tree just to taste my own juices, no opportunity to dip, skinny or otherwise, no opportunity to get blasted, count the frigging stars. So when I found out that Tom knew some guy in Denver who could get me some good paying construction-type work, I was ready to make plans.

Thankfully, though, because of some rare and honest introspection, I had to balk that first time. Why did I want to go there anyway? To work, to see Aunt Amelia like she'd asked? Yes, I could do that. But I knew, too, that that wouldn't be enough. I wouldn't make it. Within a week there'd be some kind of trial, and I'd be looking for the next exit. I needed some wind in my sails that wouldn't fade. I needed a reason to carry things through. Was there one? As I brooded over this one evening, I saw Father Beltin sitting over by himself, reading a magazine. I had to talk to somebody, figure all of this out.

He was very kind, greeted me with a smile, offered a quiet place to talk. I followed him up a very narrow set of stairs to a tiny room above the kitchen, his bedroom apparently, with a small cot, pictures of Mary, crucifixes on the wall. I told him what I could, more than I had told anyone else. He seemed concerned, but not overwhelmed. Was I in any trouble? Was I on the lamb? He liked the expression, and liked the fact that I could see he liked it.

He asked me about the state of my soul. I responded by saying that I didn't know if I had one. "Do you believe at all?" he asked. I said I was struggling with it, told him I usually felt like a bubble, rising in a tar pit. A slow release of pent-up air, black and dun puff of stickiness. At that point he rose from his chair, quickly, but without hurrying, placed his hands on my head.

I was shocked, didn't know what to do or say. He began praying earnestly, spontaneously, to Jesus. He asked that I be helped in finding my way, that I allow the light that had drawn me here to enter completely, change me. And then, just as abruptly, he was finished.

I left after some further talk, told him that, yes, I'd see him next week. And as I walked down the stairs, pictures all along the close walls, I wondered just what had happened. I felt differently in some way, lighter in my step, almost dizzy. Well, none of this could do me any harm, that much was certain. I slept better than I had in a long time that night, got up the next day to joyfully sort potatoes at the farm with Hubert. Large ones from the small.

Sounds innocent enough, but after awhile the line becomes blurred. What exactly constitutes a small potato, what a large? Both Hubert and I agreed that life was like that. The more you tried to analyze, the more you sank into the slough of despond. And yet how could one not do so?

"The rational mind isn't worth all that much, I think, at least when it comes to the important things," he said.

"You sound like my ex-girl. She was into Native America and flower essences." He smiled. Apparently not unfamiliar territory with him either.

"I guess you're right. You've got to be able to separate things, but what does Catherine say? FOLD THE WINGS OF YOUR INTELLECT." (He said this grandly.). "I want to be faithful. What else matters?"

And after a pause, "It's the flesh we're wrestling with. How do we get past these surface considerations? How can we immerse ourselves in prayer, become prayer? That's the tough question if you ask me. There are no easy answers when it comes to the daily stuff. I'm glad I'm here in any case. It's a great blessing, don't you think? To be given time and a place to find out who you really are, to find out how to live your life. That's why I came anyway."

"I came for the girls."

"Oh, come on. Hasn't this place had an effect?"

"Yeah. Too much of one maybe. I'm thinking of becoming a nun."

"And that's bad? You've been out there. You know what it's like. It gets inside you. We're all sinners to begin with, of course. But I want to get rid of all that."

"Won't help. We're made of dirt."

"Yeah, I know. Original Sin, our nature. But I want all I can get. Are you going to sign up for that Charismatic class? It's supposed to be coming around pretty soon."

"It could be a spiritual kind of doobie."

"Maybe. But maybe not too. I want to find out." And we climbed, in our mutual squats, up another mound of potatoes, bushels baskets in hand behind us.

When next I saw Father Beltin I asked him about this born-again business. He said that there were many twice-born people, people who experience dramatic conversions, and that there were those whom many called once-born: that is, people who have been faithful from childhood. A decision, or as he said he liked to put it, a movement or realization usually seems to happen somewhere along the line for all of us though. He said he didn't think it had to be a dramatic thing. For him, in fact, it was just a gradual epiphany that Jesus was the way it truly was. How could he say no to what was so obvious? And he didn't have to shout out a yes to the world either. That would be like looking at a mountain, saying, "Yes, you are mountain." Ridiculous. Absurd.

Conversion, he said meant "a turning," and that's what it is, all of your life. You turn until you become who you are, and then you are in the arms of God. This side of life or the other, it didn't matter much ultimately.

He recommended that I pray to Mother Mary, do an act of consecration, ask her to show me her Son. Persevere. Don't worry. The Lord had brought me this far. He won't let me fall away. Then he asked me more about my family background. Just open up and let Jesus do the work. Holy week was almost upon us. Wait and see what God will do.

Good Friday came with a procession and influx of people, all of us going to a special, longer-than-usual prayer service. We all went up to kiss the feet of the Crucified One, a big cross someone held. I felt a little funny. Who was this guy, really, that I should give my life to Him? God? The place where the Divine miraculously breaks through and into the stained-glass physical world, all in a collection of broken bone and skin?

"For God so loved the world." It was a wonderful story, the most hopeful one I had ever heard. Weird enough, perhaps, to be true. Besides, what other way made sense?

I looked at the people around me. They were here for the long haul, because they believed in what they were doing to the point of giving up their lives for it. They had found what they needed, were hungrily satisfied, even happy, or as happy as people can be. And they weren't stupid. I'd be a fool if I didn't give this a chance. I wanted to feel like they did, to be like they were.

On Holy Saturday evening there was more prayer, all of us stooping under a black cloth that two people held in chapel. We were going through death with Christ to rise with Him. Embracing death. And why not I figured? It seemed healthy to me.

There was something bare, pleasingly bald about the ritual. It struck me that this was where life was, again, in this Nazareth. These people were truly living, dying. Not running from life in sleek cars, dope, the fastest tennis shoes.

Easter was the biggest doings, a lamb killed and mounted especially for the occasion, an apple in its mouth. The innocent one, again, slain. Something they did every day at the Eucharistic banquet. I had to remind myself that it was, literally, God they were eating each day, the One who could not sink low enough for us, becoming even food.

That was the rap anyway, and why wouldn't it be true? That is, if God truly loved us. I had to admit it; I did like this Catholic life. There was something very profound about it; they loved, embraced irony. The sentence contradicted before completed. Not in a deconstructed way, but in a way that acknowledged Absolute Truth, in a way that took delight in life, in the mystery and contradiction of God working out His plan in a time-bound, flawed, natural world. A world filled with knuckleheads, beautiful knuckleheads like they knew they were.

There were guests from all over the world by afternoon tea. They sang their songs, did their dances. I even thanked God for the first time. For bringing me here, for having patience with me, for allowing me to see this—if He existed.

At dinner I sat with Nick and Tom. Tom brought up the renewal, and Nick along with two new female guests from Akron began talking about Jesus like they were all best pals or something. Struck me as odd, but I was interested.

"This is that Charismatic stuff, isn't it? You guys sound like you have Him over for bridge."

They laughed; "Does He like cards?" one asked the other. They both laughed, but I felt put-off. Why did they have that I didn't? And why did it make them feel so special, set apart?

Was this what it was all about, I wondered? To get to a superior place, a height you could look down from? How tenuous all this was as I looked at those smiling, beaming faces!

When we got back to the dorm late that night, later than usual, I found myself pouring over a borrowed Bible with everyone else, the Gospel of John. Each in his own bed. Even Jean-Michele had broken his out. For me it was greed, the kind Paul recommends. It had become clear to me that I was a messed up, fallen creature, and if there were spiritual gifts to get here, if I could somehow feel more completed through all of this, like Hubert, I wanted in. Nick reminded us that the Life in the Spirit course would begin a week before Pentecost.

Ascension came and went. And even though I finally managed to gird my loins and go to Confession, Communion for the first time since I was a small boy, I couldn't help but wonder why this Christ had abandoned us. Why did He have to go? Was it necessary that we play out these perilous times when the battle had already been joined, won? We could have been so much more happy had He stayed. Why did He leave? So that we could share more fully in the victory, perhaps? So that we could have a chance to fail and therefore be able to live life to its fullest intensity? Heck, I'd be willing to forgo a little freedom just to enjoy the rewards, avoid the possibility of hell.

Maybe it was as Father Tom said during his sermon the next day. God treats us with the respect due adults. We would not be happy if we had less of a life to live. He said that it is only in the standing up, in the being counted that we can be truly satisfied, live fully the life that has been given us. We are free to fail. And we will. But God will not, and that is the important thing, he said. We are called to love in His strength, through our wills. Our lives would not be worth living were that not so.

So I signed up for the stupid class, waited for some a that 'old time religion' while I washed tea time cups when it was my turn, while I sat at Catherine's feet, listening, drifting. And it was fitting preparation. Waiting is our lot in large part.

The target day for the Baptism of the Holy Spirit was Saturday, the day before Pentecost, and it couldn't arrive soon enough. My anxiety level rose, and I hoped, worried about that. Would it create problems, would it help? Would I get in the way of God acting? The plan was for each of us, the ones-to-be-anointed, to meet at a pre-arranged time in the chapel. A team of veterans would pray over us. I was to be one of the first.

Before the large icon of Jesus, his sandal strap unfastened—an invitation for those would-be more-than-John the Baptist's to tie—I knelt, and after some initial conversation, felt the three people lay hands on my head. They insisted that I praise the Lord with them whether I felt so moved or not. I did, but it seemed strange. There I was, after all, praying to some guy I wasn't even sure existed, thanking Him for what He would come back from the dead to do in my life. Here, in the boonies of Canada.

I felt foolish, but continued, mostly because I had come this far, but partly, too, because I wanted what I saw it offered. "Thank You, Jesus. Bless You, Jesus," I said until my jaws ached. But nothing was happening.

Then, finally, something did happen. I felt, no other way to describe it, a joy begin to well up inside me, and with that, the darkness, the gloom, the weight that I had been wrestling with ever since I could remember, began to slowly, surely, dissipate; or rather, I should say, it was slowly being burnt away, eclipsed by the coming of what would reveal itself as a complete interior light.

Effusive fountains of water, of Light, great handfuls of pearled praise gushing from within, welling straight up, over. My spirit, for the first time in my life, began to twinkle, dance little dances in the provinces of real joy; those quivering little beads, with my face on each wonderful one, falling to the pool beneath, each making its own splash, each rising, gelatinous: serving more curved windows of light. All the motion, the sparkle there; a kid's playful feet, rushing to splash in sunlight, water. All without the birds of denial, nothing but a fresh clear bell of blue sky, possibility, above. It was what I had always been after, this place where God lived, this house of praise, of joy.

Something had changed. A veil had lifted. And I felt the tears. But there was more: He wasn't finished yet. Intuitively, I got this sense that there was somebody else, an invisible Presence in that room. And as the team prophesied over me, the feeling grew into surety. Every question I came up with internally was answered immediately through those peoples' voices for a good ten minutes or so. And yet the team had no way of knowing what I was thinking. Someone else was there. I could actually feel Him listening, patiently answering. It was a dialogue that only He and I knew anything about.

"Your words will be the light for many," they all said, in one form or another. Of course, me being the potentially humble servant that I, by nature am, my mind ran to Shakespearean power, the lavish gifts, houses in the South of France, tall, thin women, Lamborghinis.

But the voice, again, patient, would bring me back. "All of your words for the Word, the lesser for the greater, the child for the Man."

It continued. He mentioned my parents by name, my father's baseball war picture, catcher-perfect. I was blown away, but grateful to the point of tears. Where there was nothing, He had brought life. I had changed inside, with the snap of His fingers. A one-time paralytic, rinsed, raised; pressed down, spilling over.

Why hadn't anyone told me this was possible, I wondered? Could it have been that the nuns in my youth didn't know? How could they live a Catholic life and not know about this?

Of course, at that miraculous time I had no idea as to what would be asked of me in the coming years. None of us do. I only knew that all good things were possible, inevitable. And they are—in a life abundant with joy, tears, sorrow, the long hours of good work.

I think of Mother Teresa who said that had she known what God was going to ask of her in those early days, she might not have gone through with that first step. Grim humor, but there's some truth to it. Had the reporter pressed her, I'm sure she would have said that she, at the same time, would not have had it any other way. In the end, if we are faithful, I think we will all be like chastened Peters, years after (most of the) crowing roosters, staffs in hand, all of us, humbled, quietly up the hill. Each at his own pace, each more or less alike.

We all go where we are sent because of the Sender. It is a sad life in many ways, walking through, as Catherine put it, our aging, foolish flesh, ever more aware of our need for God's mercy. But as every Christian will tell you, "It's the Sender, the Sender; it's Jesus we all look to. The perfect, the kind."

After the required hugs, mutual tears, one of the team asked me if I wanted the gift of tongues as well. "Is the Pope Catholic?" I asked, smiling, tears down my cheeks. We began in earnest, but again, it was a long process. They encouraged me to start babbling incoherently, to allow the Spirit room to take over, and I did so for awhile, but it didn't help. I was just becoming absorbed in the sound of my own voice. My mind was, as ever, still on me. The best way for me to beat that, I finally decided, was to imitate the sounds they were making, to concentrate on them. That way I could give the Spirit some space if He wished.

After ten seconds of so of imitation, it worked! The words that began to come out weren't mine anymore. Each took on its own shape, size. I felt unfamiliar clumps of blends, vowel units; unwieldy mouthfuls of syllabic groups. Each felt odd, edged, coming out; my oral cavity experiencing new demands, but there was an order to each expression as well. It was a tongue—its sound delighted me—one I had never heard before, but definitely language.

I was shocked. God, working in me! When I said, "Praise You, Jesus," this time I meant it, even though it still sounded a little odd to actually be saying that. Thanking a Man who was God at the same time. Alien stuff.

On the way back I met Greg coming up the wide chapel, I was pretty animated I guess as I gave him a loud high five, the sound echoing through the trees. Well, what about it, he wanted to know, his teeth gritting some in anticipation?

"Hey, no sweat, man. It's great. Just go with the flow. And all of that." I laughed, looked up at him and then laughed again, spreading my arms. He wanted to talk some about it, walking with me for a few steps, but I turned him back in the direction of the chapel. "Take Him out, lad. Lead with the left, the left," I said.

He threw up his arms in mock despair. "Okay, okay, I'm going."

It was about tea time when I got back, finished with my long meandering walk. And I still had to work to contain myself. I saw Suzanne, and went over to talk with her, hoping that would anchor me. We had just begun discussing this Life in the Spirit stuff, me discussing mostly, when Catherine, who had apparently been walking around the room talking to guests, came by. She sat down slowly, as her age demanded, smiled at me.

"You're ready to change the world now, Honeymooner. Well, that's good. You are on your way. The question is, can you do the laundry?"

"One foot in front of the other. I guess that will work, eh?" I winked at her, using the Canadian ending.

"Very good. But now you must climb the cross." With this she playfully shook her cane at me. "You will have the words," she said.

Then she turned, almost abruptly, and took Suzanne's hand. She began, after a short preamble, to talk about her marriage to Eddie. The two of them had lived the last fifteen years of their lives together as celibates in the community to avoid scandal. "He said it was such a little thing to give up." They both smiled. (I found out later that Suzanne had gotten an annulment before coming up here.)

"This Christian business is no place for the timid. Jesus only asks because you have it to give," she said patting the younger woman's hand. "And speak to this excited one, will you?" she said to her, nodding in my direction, giving me a playful shake with her cane. "He may need to make the connection one of these days." That puzzled me, but I was riding on too many volts right then to consider anything besides myself.

I watched her walk away, relying too much, it seemed to me, on that cane. She was getting up there. Soon the community would have to get along without her. At least on this plane. She was a saint. You could just look at her, that tough old illumined face, and tell that her will was not her own.

Suzanne and I talked about chastity. I tried to encourage her, but got a little bored with the conversation.

6.

I don't think I became immediately unpleasant. It took time. At first I would just speak a little off-key in my conversations with others, a trace of shrillness, especially when they had to do with things spiritual. I began to over-estimate just how much my conversion had changed me, how much of an impact I could make on the world.

I got Periwinkle's first missive that Tuesday after Pentecost. It was nice to hear from her. Her spryness, the spring in her pagan step. Witty, yet seemingly unconcerned, unaware of her spiritual gaffs. She wondered what the third best editor she had ever known was up to in Canada. Would I become a priest? Had they gotten to me yet?

She had moved out, in with Israel, found a nice little place in Bedford. They were living happily together, in sin, she said, trying to make a joke. She had taken up painting again as well, she said, always a good sign for her. The literary magazine we'd worked on had been out for awhile, had gotten bad reviews. It seems the two of them had requested a salary for her similar to the one given to the University's student newspaper editor. Rebuffed, they retaliated by printing the administration's rejection letter on the last page of the journal, complete with cloven-footed pig drawn underneath, an "Oink, oink" balloon.

People laughing at their own destruction: the hooves, just as I had done. Obviously, she continued, they were not going to edit the thing next year. In fact, they were contemplating moving to Texas soon, to continue their education in Austin. The change might do them both good.

I didn't want to hear all this. My past life was a bridge crossed and gone as far as I was concerned. All the sin. Too much of it was still too close. But how could I keep myself clear of it? How could I count on being faithful to the new creature I had become; ignore her for starters? That didn't make sense. I couldn't live with my head in the sand. I had to stand up, speak the truth. But I couldn't count on the fact that I could keep myself pure by just insisting in that it were so, speaking loud enough, with enough conviction to drown out the world. But on the other hand I didn't want to flirt with disaster either. I'd have to talk to Father Beltin about it.

"Old things are passed away," is what I began the return letter with. I told her about my Baptism in the Spirit, about everything that had happened, told her that I wanted to shake whatever remained of that sinful life altogether. I didn't dislike her or condemn her, told her that, that I hoped for continued friendship. I just needed time to settle into my new life, to digest all that had happened, to find a way "to tie myself to the mast, Siren."

Wanting to end the letter on a good note, I said "God grant you peace. May you know His great gifts: love and mercy, in the times you're sure to face. Your friend, James." I knew it sounded a bit grand, but on the other hand, I had no doubt that she would pay for what she was doing.

But maybe her rebellion was, in an odd sort of way, a good thing, the first step, I thought as I mailed the letter. She had always seemed so fragile in past meetings, as if rebellion were somehow beyond her capabilities. Almost a prima donna, although that was too harsh an expression, she so sadly hard put after perfection that standing on her own two imperfect feet seemed out of the question: a Priscilla, perhaps, forever-in-progress. Now she was apparently using Israel's, but maybe her own some too. God would take care of her in any case. I would keep her in my prayers.

Gradually I was moved from the farm to be the garbage collector in the main compound: incinerator detail. The only times I went to the farm now was when there were big jobs to be done: unloading hay trucks or getting wood shavings for the cow parlor. I liked my new job, got to say hey to everybody on both sides of the street, pushing my little two bicyclewheeled wagon. "Get your strawberries, tomatoes. Get your strawberries," I used to sing, to the delight of my customers. I'd say "Praise God" to everything, if I felt like praising or not, just to keep myself charged up.

People appreciated my enthusiasm. And as spring gave way to summer, I settled into my trips across the grounds, the craft and book shops across the street, the old museum, the girls' dorm, the newspaper house. I'd empty their trash cans, baskets, talk any nonsense I could think of. Each person there living his or her simple life.

Yvonne was still on the other side of the street. I found her a bigger bucket, would collect cones from all over, fill the pail which I'd set on her front porch every third day.

But soon enough, the old restlessness returned. The first "sort" of early summer helped exacerbate the situation as it involved more work than I, or most of the other guests for that matter, felt comfortable dealing with.

It started one breakfast when the word passed. Even the well-seasoned hunkered down for the siege; you could see it in their postures. I had no idea of what to expect, but judging by appearances, Saigon, Tehran came to mind. And I was not disappointed. The garages behind the orchard that were filled with boxes were only a part of the story. There was an old convent down the road, now abandoned; the place was brimming with boxes of second hand clothing, books, toys, small household items, stacks of mattresses, box springs, you name it.

It seemed like the whole community, now quite large because of the nice weather, descended on that place. Most of the donations were to go to outlying soup kitchen houses, some of those, the places mentioned on the sign next to the main house; some went to the houses of prayer, not much though, as they were more concerned with praying than with obvious acts of charity. Much went to the rural apostolate down the road in the other direction, and much was used by the community itself.

No one there owned anything. All the clothes they wore, from their wrist watches to their gym shorts—we sometimes played basketball and volleyball in the elementary school gym—had come through donations. The shirt off their backs. And if occasionally some of them proved a little too eager to reprove, you had to admit that they weren't halfbaking it with their own lives.

Tom, Nick, and I hefted huge barrels of clothing all that morning, carried mixed and sorted clothes to rooms assigned. There must have been four hundred boxes, most of them large. Nick, as ever, was the comedian, advising me to die to myself when he passed me, loaded down and sinking as I was.

"Thank You, Jesus. May I have another?" I answered several times, until I got a glance from one of the women running the show. I was angry at her unspoken reprimand, started whistling "Oh Canada," softly every time I passed her. Figured I could repent come Confession-time.

At one point Tom and I dollied a succession of very heavy boxes over to the box shop, the bindery. I hadn't even known that the place existed. But there was much about the place I learned only over time: the hay fields, the maple bush, the iconographer's hut, the machine shop, the poustinias—little cabins or rooms one could spend a day in, fast on bread and water, praying to God.

It was a great little shop. Old books were re-bound here, stacked, mailed out. Seems they had a small business going, were in touch with antique booksellers throughout Canada. Earning money that would go to the poor or toward buying insulation.

(There had been quite a hub-bub about that. Should they be one with the poor of the region and not have any, or should they get some and put it in to save money, and thus be good stewards? Catherine got out-voted I guess, though apparently she did have veto power. It was installed.) No stone was left unturned by these guys. They even reused their large envelopes, old string.

We hauled boxes until we collapsed on the grass, then got up and hauled some more. Catherine saw me sling a barrel over my shoulder, encouraged me with, "That's right. Put your back into it." She was a sensitive woman, if out-spoken, and I'm sure she didn't mean to sound like a slave master. She was delighting in my willingness to do God's work. But it began to bother me as we approached the afternoon. I began to think about the outside world. Maybe I should leave soon, get started.

It was quite an operation, though. You had to stand in awe. Women, sewing, re-beading blouses, needle and eye under the early summer sun. Woman and men guests, doing whatever was asked of them. Everybody shuffling boxes, sorting, out on the hot lawn.

Tom set one down, sweat glistening on his furrowed brow. "Man, nobody works this hard in the outside world."

"Give these women the next war, I say."

He said he wished Jean-Michele were still around to enjoy the festivities. He had left the day before, barely leaving a wake in the water, and that was not rare. So many people now, in and out. A quick hug and an address and they were down the road, you after your job for the day. It was kind of sad, actually, people exchanging addresses, most knowing somewhere inside of them that they would never make it over to their friend's part of the country: this one or that. You had to figure how close of a friend you were. Should you offer or not? There was nothing more painful than watching someone collecting information from a reluctant or surprised pal. Everyone was charitable and all, but nobody missed that. Tom asked me how long I was staying.

"Ah, I don't know. I suppose I should start thinking about my vocation soon enough. What about you? How's your mom?"

"The nuns next door still look in on her, but I've really got to get back soon. It's dead summer now, and work has started to pick up. A friend of mine and I've got a small business going. Inner-city house repair, at reasonable rates. That kind of thing."

"Charity work whether you like it or not." He smiled, shook his head in assent.

"Are you going to look up your aunt in Denver when you go? If you do, I've got that buddy I told you about there, a high school friend who could always use a hand. Construction-type work, remember? The money's good. Let me give you his address before I go, anyway. I'll write him."

I thanked him, said I might take him up on the offer.

Then it was back to the mines.

By afternoon tea things had slowed down, at least for us. The women were still busy as bees, tireless. I thought about vocation. What would it be like to be a priest? I had to admit I was always a pulpit kind of guy. Still, you had to be such a company man. Then it occurred to me that people were always talking about that possibility with Greg or Nick, but nobody ever did so with me. I knew it was childish but why hadn't anyone ever asked me? It became a burr in my saddle, stayed there until my appointment with Fr. Beltin that evening after vegetables.

"Well, it's something to think about," he said puffing on his pipe, thinking about it. "You would make a fine priest. Naturally, I would recommend it." Both of us smiled. He was a good-looking guy, taller than me by a couple inches, thin, with his hair going white, about 45 or so. He could have married had he wanted to, been successful in the world. "It's not an easy life, but a rewarding one. Priests are called to be witnesses, prayers really. And that's true for all Christians but especially so for a priest. It's a special calling, to be an instrument. To become clear, not a speck of dust. " Here he got quiet, a little inward. But then he picked up.

"And then of course, there's the Eucharist," he said laughing, spreading his arms open wide, getting up from his chair, conveying clearly how much it meant.

He had an open, intelligent face. You could tell that he had long been praised for his ample gifts, and if he did seem awfully sure of himself to me, to one who wasn't, I couldn't really complain. Just then I was the beneficiary. I would have given a lot to be like that, still would: sure of myself, holy, large in some way. But I see now that it's not my way. I'm not an effusive, expansive type—unless I'm in my cups.

In many ways this community life was all that I could have asked for. It has the earmarks of being my vocation. It offered prayer, challenge: intense personal work, consolation, a chance to really be there for people. And there was always something going on.

That weekend, for example, someone set up a volleyball net in the large space between the sheds and St. Paracletus, in front of the pumps. Staff members, Jim and Patrick, a few priests, visiting and regular, male and female guests, all of us engaging in good sport. The laughs, the banter, the poor unfortunate who, always on such occasions, tend to dominate because of his or her skill, trying to delicately (or not so delicately) assert strategy, technique.

You can always see the burden on their faces. Moving people around in the nicest possible way, the quiet looks, almost unnoticed when someone messes up. To the priests' credit, they knew just when it was time to call it a day. The fun had peaked, as attitudes were just beginning to get ragged. Everyone left, sweaty and mostly happy.

Many of us went swimming just to cool off. Eighty-five degrees, no black flies, and a clear river in front of the house. Greg and I had a leisurely time on some inner tubes, drifting far out near the center of the river until motorboats and skiers made us retreat. The women had their own swimming place farther down, across the house. We lamented that we could hardly ever see them, decided to eventually pillage town, eat chocolate.

We stopped up at St. Joe's, and Mary Kay invited us into their house, across the lot from the apostolate for a "beverage." (I've never personally used that word.) They offered us some tea, talked to us about the plight of the rural folk around there. Some lived way up in the bush, had no electricity, no plumbing or running water. But they all had t.v.'s though, generators, Janine added. Figure that. We all laughed.

As I looked out the front window toward the reeds and recesses of the river, Janine answered our questions, spoke a little about herself. She had been a speed skater, had been on the Canadian Olympic team in fact, but found her life wanting. On current vacations she still pursued her athletic bent, went camping in the National State park about a hundred miles away, lived on what food she could find there. She'd go white-water rafting with a friend, another staff member.

Even though she was forty of so, she still had an athlete's walk, the slight jerk that demanded more of her step than it was inclined to give. She was nice looking, and I wondered how lonely this kind of life could get.

"Loneliness is part of the package, you know. It's part of any vocation. It's Christ on the cross: suffering. Embrace it and you're free. Avoid it and you die anyway. It's either death or death. One brings God glory, the other brings nothing. Not much of a choice, eh?" she laughed.

"You can't avoid it, so it becomes a question of what you do with it." At this she looked me quickly, deeply in the eyes, as if she were looking for something, as if she were measuring my depth to see how much pain I had endured, how far I had progressed. I averted my eyes quicker than I would have liked, in fear of giving myself away, but it was too late. I lived far closer to the surface than any real growth would have allowed for and felt ashamed, angry because of it. I was upset, too, in knowing what she'd done, felt summarily dismissed.

She, however, didn't seem to give the whole episode a second thought, continued. "There's a slow pain you come to, have to go through every day. You can feel yourself being refined, and because of that, you take all you can take; and then the next morning you begin again, take some more. You become 'a living sacrifice of praise.' And then one day, as Catherine says, it's not so much for you anymore. It's for others.

"I've seen her do it, take on other people's pain. She calls it a joyful crucifixion. Have you ever seen that statue of Saint Teresa of Avila, the one with her in ecstasy, with the pierced heart? That's what the Bee means, I think. A painful ecstasy. Sometimes the Lord floods her with that joy, and the loneliness seems to die a little. But it's always there, her cross."

"Can't she just pray it away? Why does she have to take on other's pain? Jesus has already done that, hasn't he? I find that if I praise loud enough, long enough, that the Lord takes away the pain," I said. Greg looked back out the window again, still listening.

"Then who benefits?"

I pushed my hand through my hair. "But what about us? What about my life? Don't I get a life too?"

"So what if you are obliterated?" she said, looking right at me, smiling. It was too much. I hemmed and hawed a little bit, eating some jam bread. Then we left.

"Some pretty heavy stuff," Greg said. "Want to set ourselves on fire tonight? We could be Buddhists. Yeah." But we were both too absorbed to talk much. We grabbed a few Canadian candy bars from the General Store, headed back.

About five hundred yards from the compound we saw Daoud cut up a dirt road. Greg, being the sociable guy he was, called out to him. I wasn't so crazy about Daoud. I knew it was his Palestinian Arab ways that I couldn't get past, but there they were. He meant well, but would say whatever was on his mind, if you wanted to hear it or not. (Most times l didn't.)

Once I had to work with him on the farm. I had been cutting the meat from a cow's head, as ordered, after it had been slaughtered. Whenever he passed, he would jump right in, start telling me four ways to do it better. That was all I needed, another boss. Finally, after too much of it, I had to explain to him the different customs on this side of the globe. People ask for help before you give it. I showed him my face, told him to stay out of it.

He met us with warmth, cried out, "Jesus, where are You?" to the skies above us. (He used to do that all the time: as he walked to the outhouse at the farm; while picking beans. He'd stand in the middle of a row, lift his head, extend his arms and do so.) He was an interesting case, a very bright fellow. There was no denying that. At twenty-one he'd just finished his dissertation in mathematics, written in French. He said he found Canada very beautiful, and I admired him for his youthful enthusiasm, his obvious spiritual experience—at times at night he'd come over to my bed and make a sign of the cross on my forehead, bless me. Some of the other guys found that a little annoying, but I didn't mind, despite my reservations. They could line up as far as I was concerned.

"You know, Catherine came here with nothing. A good story really. Like Peter out on the water."

"Yeah, but I'm a little tired of Catherine. Catherine this, Catherine that. St. Catherine. Maybe we should wait until she dies." Greg wanted to talk about Palestine. What was happening over there?

I didn't really care, wanted to be alone. So I begged off at the next green fork in the road. Daoud blessed me, and I was elsewhere.

It looked like a snowmobile path, with its high grass, all the birds chirping. I was happy the black flies had come and gone, and enjoyed myself immeasurably in the generous spacing of the trees, walking over old pine needles on the busy green floor of the forest. Up and down the hills, it struck me that this was the only time that I had really been alone since I got here, at least for any extended period of time. No one to meet, no place to go. I sat and rested on a fallen tree, just to appreciate it, a deer, not two hundred feet from me, eating, watching.

I passed a few intersecting paths as I walked that distance, winding with the road, saw an old deserted cabin down a slope ahead. There wasn't much to it, 1947 newspapers in the deserted rooms, what was left of an old woodburning stove, the green finding its way through patches of wall, porch flooring. Entropy, I figured. Praise God. It got us all. And more, I took it as a warning. The spiritual life, unattended.

That got me to thinking about the prophecy. What would happen to me? Would I be a writer, a teacher, or just a talker maybe? "Your words for the Word." Such a deal, I thought—for him.

He could have them all of course, my words, and gratefully. It wasn't like I was doing much with them. I did hope though that he'd exert His influence in some continuously profound manner before I took to yammering. I'd blow it in a minute, given my past performances. It would be nice to have some positive effect on someone for a change.

The longer I stood in that room, though, the more the place began to have an affect on me. Just how completely had the Lord changed me anyway? I certainly hadn't been very kind to Daoud. That depressed me some. It was clear that I was as doomed as ever to spend all my time inside my own sorry rooms, like everybody else on the planet, whatever I did. An iffy voice inside my too mortal skin. How many of us have a holy enough perspective to move beyond the confines of our fallen nature anyway I wondered, beyond genetics, influences, bad food? All the things that could turn a weak Christian away from the narrow way. Maybe I'd just wait until I was as old as Catherine before I said anything. That would be one way.

I resolved to try and live within the small silence of who I was, to try and find my joy there. If nothing else that might keep me from mistaking myself for Jesus. And it wasn't a bad room as rooms probably went. There was a view, occasionally good company.

But all humor aside, I was worried. How was I supposed to keep the joy? I couldn't go around reciting the Rosary every minute of the day. I was thankful for what He'd done in my life, profoundly so, but would it last? How could I help make that happen?

Finally I decided that I might as well set up a nice little table in here, a few lamps, stock the shelves with some good reading while I prayed and waited to get the answers. It would be a long siege. In the meantime I could lay low, and a nice recliner, my tongue for a footstool.

I discussed all of this with Fr. Beltin that night and was grateful for his laughter. Don't worry, he told me. Jesus loved me. He wouldn't let me slip through His fingers. Then he suggested poustinia. (I had heard distant talk about the experience. Tom and Nick had gone, and once Nick got up after lunch at the main house to give the word he had received to the community. Something about God's mercy, I didn't really remember.) I would get to take a day off of work; that was the best thing about it, would take a loaf of bread and a jug of water to a little cabin. There I would spend 24 hours alone, in prayer and fasting, seek God.

The cabin was out in the boonies, even for this place. Just out of range of the younger male staff's main quarters, a hay field between us. Inside my little home-away-from-home-away-from-home there was a wood-burning stove, thin cot, a table and chair, a Bible, a four foot high red cross hanging on the wall with a crown of thorns looped over it.

I didn't really know what to expect from all of this, messed around a bit with the fire, kindling and paper stacked next to the stove, just the one room, mortar and thick logs, bounced on the bed for a bit. Taking my time, I read the whole Gospel of St. John, tapped my fingers on the desk after that. Finding a pad and a pencil in the drawer, I took to drawing sunny faces. Got even more restless.

I began feeling like a little kid, like I should have had some jacks and a ball to bounce on the floor. So here I was again, with myself, my boon companion. "Hi, James." "Hi." We got along fine.

I went outside. Felt like taking a long walk, but then figured that, since I was here, I really should do the tour. I flopped horizontal on the hard bed, said a Rosary, and felt, perhaps because of that, something come over me, an expectancy. For what I couldn't really say, so eventually I let it go, decided to ignore the feeling. Eventually, even though it was the middle of the day, I slept.

The sleep itself was uneventful, at least as I remember it, but as I began to come out of it, I saw her—the Queen of Heaven. The most beautiful woman I have ever seen. In white robe, gold trim. She didn't say anything, but had such a profound sense and look of peace and meekness to her that she didn't have to. She just stood there, praying, not looking at me, smiling her hidden, slight smile of complete faith.

Why she came in this dramatic way, I didn't know. I don't even remember if my eyes were opened or closed, if I were completely awake; I only knew that I was not sleeping.

Maybe she came just to show she was, perhaps, that she would always be with me. I don't know, but it is true that she has never left.

As the dung-beetle said, "It was no dream." The peaceful effects, fruit, stayed with me in the long twilight, and beyond, as I prayed, more easily this time. Washed in the miracle of her ordinariness, I took quiet delight in the good wood of the cabin, the floor, windows, the stars. There was something wonderfully worthy in the dirt that made up the planet outside. I squatted down outside and cupped my hands to hold some. How cool the soil was, as night settled in. I realized how creation answers, always, to the call to life.

I wanted to be like that dirt. I wanted to be there for God's hand, for any seed He had for me. And the grasses. There was great peace in their movement. Why had I been missing that? My heart overflowed with a simple, profound gratitude. This was all God's. He had made it, and it all spoke of Him in some way. Every step along the path. And the path itself, all of it taking me to Him. How could I ever be separated?

And Mary, there, helping at every turn. But I wondered, the more I thought of her: why in white? Whenever I had seen her, in grade schools or in churches, she had always been dressed in blue.

Eventually, though, it was time for sleep, so I bicycled my legs several times through the cool sheets just to feel the cold give way gradually to warmth, like I used to do as a kid.

Even this, I remember smiling.

The next morning at lauds I was still mulling over the blue and white question when this guy I had never seen before, from outside the community—a rare thing—brought in a big statue of Mary into chapel. White, gold piping; he had been carrying it around the world: Our Lady of Fatima. I was amazed. A miracle of coincidence. In my face.

I excitedly told Father on the way to breakfast, but he didn't seem to think it any big deal. (He probably didn't want to encourage a neophyte in his visions.) I was kind of angry that he didn't share my enthusiasm, though. And as I began making my rounds with my silly little cart, I wondered what the heck I was still doing in this place anyway. Hadn't I gotten my commission? Wasn't it time for me to go out and meet the world. Sure a lot of people stayed on and became staff members, but that wasn't for me.

My life in the world had not been a great success, so I felt like that's where I wanted to go, that's what I had to do. Make that work. Nick was taking off the following week, so I talked to him about it and decided that that would be as good a time as any. I called Tom's buddy to get the go-ahead and then had to live with the anticipation a possible future can generate. The prospects kept me adrenalized, impatient, but I kept a lid on it, went about my duties like a grim storm trooper.

I wanted badly to change for the good, but would have had to become something else to do it. I was, I realized for that moment, no help, and I felt that increasingly in the succeeding days. Only God could do that, probably taking a lifetime in the process.

That first night I talked to Suzanne about my funk. She nodded, said that she knew what I was talking about. It was like something was missing, even with the presence of Christ in our lives. Maybe the incompleteness in all of us until we meet Him in glory. For her, she said, it was easiest to place it within the metaphor of her broken marriage. The wound that ate Charlestown, that would not go away. It was a blessing, she believed, that was sure; but, at the same time, it reminded her of St. Teresa: "Lord, if this is how you treat your friends, no wonder you have so few of them."

She laughed at that, pulled down on her scarf.

She talked about her past, her real estate business. She had cleaned up re-doing old Victorian houses, reselling them. But five years into her marriage, it had become increasingly clear that her husband was gay. She'd found different male shoes around the house. That takes a lot from a woman, she said. To know that you're not enough.

But God was merciful; all things worked to the good. Again with the scarf. She said a woman needs to feel special. She needs to feel like the place she's chosen to expend all her love is worth it.

7.

The day Nick and I were ready to go, as we sat through the prayer for the travelers after breakfast, I couldn't get something out of my mind that one of the staff people, Tom, an old guy from Brooklyn, had told me the day before. We had been engaged in the tedium of bringing boxes of bottles into the basement of the residence building, St. Goupil's, up at St. Joe's. He picked up on my sighs, the dragging of my feet. "There's no glamour in the Gospel," he said, walking ahead.

That really struck me. I was going back to the world. I'd have to get up each morning, bale hay and hoist boxes whatever the work, whether I liked it or not. And I would have to find a way to please God, rejoice, as I was doing it. Would I be up for it? I didn't know. I tried to take my solace in the fact that God would be there, that He would see me through.

I sat at Fr. Bob's table at breakfast, said my emotional good-byes in the basement, fine handshakes and hugs. And having gotten the numbers and addresses of everyone I would try to keep in touch with, I looked one last time to make sure I had the address and phone number in Denver and set out.

On the bus with Nick I felt a fire build as the miles rolled beneath our feet; I felt high as a Japanese kite in Central Park, the wind and bright sun driving me, past the string even—nothing but the Spirit of God pushing me forward, deciding what would happen next. I felt so energized I could hardly stay in my seat. And even when I did manage to calm myself, I couldn't take the smile off of my face. Here I was, immersed in God's own Spirit, and I would make a difference. He loved me intimately; I felt washed in that love. How could it be otherwise?

I immediately began thinking of some leadership conferences I had seen in a newspaper up at the farm. Maybe I could move into the downtown area of Denver, start up a ministry with young people on drugs. I certainly had had enough experience. Of course I would have to clear it with the diocese.

But what if the Bishop didn't have the gifts of the Spirit? What if he were locked up into the old ways and insisted on dried-out, time-worn legalisms, ineffective ecclesial position politics? Maybe I'd just have to go it alone. Pamphlets on the sidewalk, that sort of thing—the thought of it made me smile. God would be with me.

For some reason the two of us, Nick and I, began to talk about fasting. I wanted to start when I got settled, for one month at a time maybe. He smiled in that generous way of his, suggested that the bigger the attempt, the bigger the fall. I concurred, but knew as well that no big thing was ever done without a big effort. The Lord had work for me to do, and it would be ingratitude not to gird my loins and get out there. What was worse than lukewarmness? So I kept my own counsel the rest of the way. Let the fire fall. I'd be ready.

We stopped at Woodstock, Ontario, to visit some Ukrainian monastery Nick was onto. It was a sad sight in many ways. A few old boys who only spoke Ukrainian and a younger man, about forty who seemed to have been sentenced there by the Vatican, occupied this huge empty farm. The old guys were holy though, childlike, cute even with their big, happy cherry cheeks, glasses. One beamed at me as he offered soup, even though neither of us understood the other.

The house had three stories and rooms upon rooms to spare, a big chapel as well, too big for a monastery it seemed to me with its statues, unused sanctuary. Three tabernacles graced that area. There were rows and rows of votive lights, a tall dome above, room for about 150 people, and there they were, five old boys, singing their office in the choir loft. No one on the main church floor.

They had a lot of land outside, too, though they had only planted a medium-sized garden. Apparently they were waiting for the bigger order to decide what to do with them next.

It seemed so absurd, metaphorical. The old church, good, but wasted, going, unused as it was by younger folk who spoke only

MTV, who went about an entirely different life, trying to find the right Michael Jordan tennis shoes to wear.

Like joyful nincompoops those old monks stayed there, waiting for young people who would never come, waiting even past the hope of that. Because they were put there ultimately. It struck me as holy, odd, still does. How few come to the obedient voices that could really help them. At that time, though, I wondered, puffed up as I was, if maybe they weren't out of date. Maybe that was the problem; maybe they needed to do some demographic research, discover behavioral patterns.

The younger man, however, was a different ball of wax. He had tried to make waves, changes, and was sentenced here until the order could figure out what to do with him. Vatican II had charged him up, or so it seemed. He was hungry for it, change, stalked around the place with Nick and me, telling us all about it.

He could have devoured a lion.

We spent a couple of days there, me mostly stewing, and then it was on to the Cleveland Greyhound Station where we split up. Glad hands and addresses. It was good to be back and to celebrate I decided. I'd try and call an old girlfriend, see what she was up to, for lunch maybe, before I split westward. I picked up the phone, but then had a change of heart. What was the point, really? I'd pray for her, for all of them; but why open old wounds. I had a job waiting for me, a new evangelical life to start.

Forming St. Anthony

From the Assidua of St. Anthony

1. Here Begins the Prologue to the Life of Blessed Anthony

Ferdinand, sitting with the bulls,
swore he could hear daisies growing, the stretch,
how they sighed through the expanding weave
of crackling green sleeves; muscular—procreant as God.
Wherever he went, blossoms, dewy cups toasted
trees with allelus; folds of wind-blown fabric.

He could, on sunny days, perch a kitchen chair
in river shallows: the music of the spheres,
moving in wet creases, the noise, in leaping
adolescent streams. Orchestrated chaos lifted him,
heaven's antechamber, shining stones.

And when the world pulled him back from itself,
it was always the unexpected motion
that unnerved him: a friendly dog jumping up his legs.
But that, he knew, was what he was here for:
each moving human face, voice, its story!

As the Wounded Hand, blood-red, passed over
every plant, seeped into rays, forming colors, discs—
its shadow roused Ferdinand to the way we must take:
justice. He lived there, where nothing exists

for itself. Grateful—dust, he spoke for, out of:
other people always, in the end, making us real.

A difficult, heavy body pressured his breathing:
Jesus's hand always on his shoulder—a print
in his dust as he proceeded, following
at a slower, challenged pace:

apt metaphor, he thought, a bear on the scent,
doing his slow dance among the trees!

2. Concerning the City of Blessed Anthony

Ulixbone, pirated son of Ulysses, its wide river
mouth sounding the future: "Brazil."
It was a good place for a boy, the wind
like sea-going cogs down bone-narrow
Atlantic streets; the Cathedral, guarding its honor,
its necessary usurpation.

The family house made its shade generous,
boys yelling down streets while they still
had the time. Ferdinand grew there, wise
to the noises, in the passing fable that is this world:
people, his friends, as ghostly and transient
as they were real.

Palm trees, busy as maids; the sky, blue enough
to matter. But his pals and their voices,
they went to a more permanent home after dark
reclaimed those streets. His parents would follow,
no doubt, he knew that, he as well.
What was here—was not his, ever.
So he waited.

The world would open up in front of him,
as it had done for others. He would stow
what he could in books below, learning domestic
lore as he went—what escaped him
catching the kitchen help.

2. Concerning the City of Blessed Anthony

Priests, the body of St. Vincent of Saragossa,
provided a larger, cathedral point of view:
birds—gold-fringed, violet, flew up, their wings
echoing, turning the vellum under stained glass.
He felt born in incense, vestments,
had become a paten.

His teachers kept his eye on every mathematical
line and plane. What rooms best fit? Where
did his excitement lead? Satisfied days
left him spent: his father's last dollar, but for what?
On some days all he had was the length
of his own stride.

Tomorrow was not his concern.

3. How He Entered the Order of St. Augustine

Under gilded billows, the white heft of futures
he couldn't see, Ferdinand would scourge
infidels down side streets. The gleam of the ocean,
the commerce of masted ships, opened waters
until it was boyhood itself, in the end,
that sailed calmly away.

Puberty, the rest of his life came down,
as it does for everyone: his capacity for sin;
error named him, whatever the strength in his hands.
Vanity, emptiness ruled everywhere like kings.
So one day, he decided to put
the flesh's parade behind him.

In a winter sun, under fewer leaves,
what passed for this life blew down bare streets,
incomplete as history, measuring him
in a cold beauty: the Eden which was not here.
He and his friends could talk until Tuesday,
about anything, dance to music they could not hear.
(Such chirping—it would've had more value
had it been parsed to pure sound.)

People's everyday business, too, mimed only
what they wanted to be. Earthly joy was here,
yes, but it was dust too; and who wanted

to spend his time on trade that didn't matter,
where nothing could hold its price?

Quiet, and then graced action: the hands of God
somewhere inside, holding up his own—
that was what he wanted.

Augustine's shout, a gleaming monastery
set aside for a king, called out like heaven
in white tile, walls. So Ferdinand traded the poverty
he knew for the poverty he didn't, became a type:
the faceless man of God—though his friends
never quite seemed to get that. They would crowd
the sacristy with talk, walk him to his cell!

They'd never waned in God's silence, it seemed—
like the moon—down to each separated bone,
the white disc windowed there on nicked sheen,
a wooden table; just the desert wind outside.

No, he would just have to leave his beating heart:
his family's native place—which was fit.
He had to serve the Lord where he didn't matter,
exist any more; he needed to be sheltered
by unfamiliar contours, another shore, by masts
that had never spoken his or his family's name.

God would have to eat him as He did the rocky shore,
until he was all pock and quiet substance,
ready to do absolutely nothing for his Lord.

4. How He Progressed in Virtue and Learning in Coimbra

Mice raced him down the halls of his life.
He was, he hoped, like them, too small to notice,
to be of any real use; the Bible telling him that virtue
wears a coat of no colors. And so he could finally
occupy his room—because, on a good day,
he was the only one of him there.

These were the days scripture writes on the soul:
easing off flakes of lambskin; ecstatic glyphs
which carve one's place, the everything that comes after.
Ferdinand had become a fife, one bright note
in a Wind that dipped and rose his life.

One puzzle piece, then the next: the truths knowledge
can obscure, this world filled with what contains it.

He valued his anonymous mates: true trope,
because it was always actions that finally spoke;
and these had been reduced to silence, pure
movement; they had nothing, really, to give him—
next in a line, heaving white, at the noisy ropes,
giving to what they still might become.

5. How, Moved by the Desire of Martyrdom, Blessed Anthony Entered the Order of Friars Minor and Concerning His Change of Name

Lord Peter Infante unfolded, smoothed the edges
of his shroud—Moroccan friars: Berard, Peter,
Accursius, Adiutus, and Otto, Catholic sighs
which forever sign this world.

It was clear what Ferdinand had to give: now
or more slowly, after all, what did it matter?

Outside the pearl-shine of Coimbra's gates,
these dusty Franciscans worked fields
whose chaff had given them form. Not learners—
that, for Ferdinand, entirely to the good:
these "humans" who could only read
the Scripture in their lives,
begging at the door of this world.

"Brothers, I would take the leaves, the cold night
for a habit, because comfort to me is a bile,
a cloak I cannot wear, nor share."
The friars took him—
because they took everyone.

They hopped around him like birds, arranging
rags! Ferdinand rejoiced in the absurdity—

then paled, thinking of kin, each
coming with position, shining clothes.

The brothers, though, since they had
no resources, didn't care—they named him
"high sounding." (Well, if irony were with him,
he decided, who could stand against?)

Not time, which would have him walk
an alien earth. He would be who he preached.
Like that other earth, its air, he would let
the Son of Man go where He chose.
You could call him Anthony if you liked.
You could call him resonance or raisons.
That world turned because it was truly world.

6. How He Went to Morocco and Concerning His Return

Morocco: he'd spent all his life
imitating this truth. His holy flight from it
would soon be ended.

But God is the face of this world,
keeps His own counsel; He would have Anthony
stay awhile—his small hand, his red chips!

All that winter in Africa, sickness
blew over him: an answer, prone, sand scripting
its message. It slept every night next to him:
"Who do you wait on, martyr?
His name or your own? What crown
can be had at your hands?"

He felt his hollow teeth start to soften, ache
as he flagged; his wages: sand in the sack
that surrounded his heart—it found his lungs,
grains of insistent doubt. (Death would be
a longer battle than the one he had imagined.
Its say is vast, and he had
to endure its half-truths.)

There was no escape, even as he crawled
back after winter—having to find his life
on the earth now, the search as home.

Pilgrim's Gait

Deranged, he stumbled along what seemed
a beach, sand and sea, found what might have been
a boat, broken rudder, a sirocco:
too much sand, a future that didn't need him.
The weather took him to Sicily as it happened,
General Chapter: the large doors of this world,
open—all he had, gone.

Coming clear in stages, he wavered
like the approaching coast, rejoiced at this
bizarre invitation. Friars everywhere—
like driftwood, or bugs, hopping the beach;
so he followed there, collapsing, got up.

He was of earth now, a browned leaf, making
ready for the two pyres that eat our bones,

the next thing.

7. How He Came to Romagna and How He Lived There

The sun, through a noisy shuffling
of spotted green leaves, fast hands overhead,
disturbed him. They rattled like tin,
irritated under oaks, pine. The last kid picked:
he was happy, but with an edge,
in the great exhalation.

Friar Gratian's beefy, grinning face
chose him (long ago). Chubby finger
to pressed lips—yes, he would take in this
last foreign soul, teach him to abandon
irksome charity, at least, to eat without a fuss.

As for Anthony, he was happy to leave
learning's unblinking eye, every spiritual lead,
to walk the dogged behind, silent with birds
who wove their good counsel in and out of the air.

They made it to Romagna, Anthony collecting
what he could find of himself, 400 meters
above the tiresome sea—in Christ, who spoke
each new place and time, who chose,
just now, more water.

Pilgrim's Gait

A fellow friar hauling stones, Anthony watched
the man jerk each landward, away from sea,
building a wall, a cell, to keep out the world;
and needing to burn the past he had fashioned,
Anthony begged for it, a life small enough
to take him, make him other.

Friar Grace was happy to give away
his only plan. So Anthony, feasting on his sins,
began in earnest, falling down for hunger,
the desires of his flesh whispering him on,
completing his spine; the only sound, the distant,
inescapable surf. It was a slim enough
martyrdom—perhaps the only kind.

The friar who had to carry him back
some days after prayer watched as his old toes
reach for the ground, as if he'd taken,
or was taken by, its full measure.

It was only in the suffering of another world
that he could find home.

Did angels attend him there, offer Eucharist?
Did he own their life-giving names?
In the Wounds, the hurling sea, his friends
and family were the threads of grace
which spoke his name: so many, reaching—
so many hands, his own.

8. How His Learning was Noted by the Friars

Discovered—and interrupted, he was asked
to read, instruct barely lettered priests,
the road to Forli.

So he talked some, let the birds do the rest.

Asking the Dominicans to address his abashed,
the Superior could get neither them
nor the Franciscans to deliver what they knew,
or what they didn't—before their betters.

So Anthony, the last man, was picked again,
to open his reserve: into a modest umbrella,
one hoped, or perhaps a soft rain—something at least
equal to the time spent.

He did.

Anthony knew the creases, the causation of leaves.
In him knowledge's last resource was words,
because it came first. He delighted,
like a boy on a ledge, in everything that roved beneath,
everything above. Prayer was his flag, his hat;
it was his friend, had so completely
become his life that his talk created him.

Pilgrim's Gait

And so this man, known only for his quiet
kitchen completions, opened scripture so gingerly
you could hear his fingertips speak to the pages.
Trees spoke softly there, the combing breezes,
Tuesdays.

You could hear that one bird sing: sure, alone.

Words didn't matter so much at that point;
each one was at home, as was its echo. There was
nothing to understand. You were where
you were supposed to be. Questions came later.

9. Concerning His Preaching in Romagna and on the Conversion of Heretics

The minister took hold of his hands
as if they were made of pewter. Here learning
lived: cows on a hillside, in strong peasant ale;
learning as it ought to be—a part of the creation
it unfolds, makes in the keeping: God's voice,
syllable by uttered syllable.

Anthony was sent—to speak people alive again,
to see Church in the disputations of flowers.
Obedience lead him wherever he went,
his quiet prayers dictating weather as he knelt
near streams, found company under wet trees.

Cities and castles rose—gratefully—
beyond him, in scrambles of children,
in the day-long smell of hay. He reacted, spoke
what he had to say, to one person or to many,
to a dog in the street. (His fasting had made him
wide enough to hang his shirts on a line.)

Reaching Rimini, his robe attracted Cathars;
and in them he saw himself—again, perhaps,
in Portugal, full of a good spirit, self, ready to claim
a prize that was not yet his. These, too,
would ride that shine into paradise,
if it were there or not.

So he called them back to morning mists,
to milky grasses, to the simplicity of motion:
children for God's sake! Each was His speech!
To serve the people they only needed
to sit down in the middle of their own smell.

Their sin was their home.

He asked if they'd ever seen a child
at something new, delighting in its properties—
the very thing, a revelation. God played here,
in their ridiculous neighbors! And weren't
those absurdities their own? If there were no
physical world, how could they see the Spirit
move the trees, their gaunt brothers,
alive now, laughing above them!

And what were they at before they sought him?
Isn't that how it has always been for us?
Up to the grunt in good work: mouths
who would feed—them, finally!
Those whose passion is great enough, doesn't
that always start in what is simple, here?

One Bononillo, who just saw years of his life
vanish, stood speechless before this patience—
ease: a man who lived where and what
he spoke, a man acquainted with grief.

His penance: to make a sand castle
and pronounce it good, then wait for rain
to wash him clean. And from that moment
he sought to live in each one, obeying
every foolish priest, right up until his end.

10. Concerning His Fame and the Efficacy of His Preaching

Friars lay scattered in a circle around him, ash
they might still become.

Petals outside clapped in the breeze.

Anthony could stop time: leaves
would cease their sway, the Curia become still life,
pure potential; a basket of flowers
became a basket of flowers. And so how
could he keep the sun-lit casements open,
the Pontiff wondered, dust floating
on each of their given names?

The learned, waxed in position, called him "Ark,"
marveled that a country vegetable
could so adapt to spiritual things; and the poor,
those more in line with heaven's soup kitchen,
were stunned as all of heaven seemed to wait
for their words, next move.

Social pork, since it did not matter to Jesus,
didn't matter to him. He responded, offered
what came. Reading hearts was just reading bodies.

Pilgrim's Gait

He never paused for inducements, because
they belonged to someone else; he lived in footprints,
in a world that made no sense at all,
at least none to him.

He watched it fall in berries and nuts
at everybody's feet: a kind of a dance, the world
and its motion—the rhythm of Jesus.

11. How He Came to Padua and Preached There

In a sodden Basilica, the littlest tramp
insisted the friars, even as they lay him down,
feed on disrupting grief—his final dark spade.
Brokenness gave that seepage meaning,
Francis choosing Anthony's tongue
to continue wasting everything built.

And so, obedient, along the knife-edge
of his perpetual sin, Anthony put down
flaking lambskin, his white Sundays.
He would walk, instead, every road to Padua—
where leaning houses held up the nightly cold,
where every woman learned to try and make do.

He preached both ale and abstinence,
filling that winter with peasant-worthy draughts:
the snow, bare branches of the saints,
crystals created to solve every cold.

When Lent came, he preached streets non-stop,
a forty day libation—a penance so obvious
that everyone had to listen; no easy task, he owned,
since his earthly weight worked against him.
He had so little control, upending tables:
legs, bloated as all human zeal.

Pilgrim's Gait

He would sit down to gather himself,
keep preaching, as if the pause had been planned.
Before he had finished, he would spend
all their coins, teach them the ABCs
that none of us ever quite learns, listen
to the same confessions, thinning, perhaps,
a little—two heavy heads against the screen.

12. Concerning the Devil's Persecution and the Miracle of Light

Night offered its incipient repose—
until a rush of clumsy elephantine
peanut-smelling snorts hemmed around his tent,
offering its eternity spent poking every lollard—
and just how do fallen angels recreate anyway?
There are no Bahamas in hell, after all,
no cold beer, no sway of lantern or ocean.

His is a life of nocturnal insinuation,
cliché gestures, each mocking him in the delivery,
each a spot on the mirror of his mind, strategies
from earlier times, no one watching them
begin to fray at the edges.

His women, too, each with her own Victorian
corset; and at the bottom of an ill-fitting
dresser drawer: the last saw—retribution!
Enumerations until the end of time,
all of it delivered, on some level, with a yawn,
all of it done to death centuries before,
none of it with any life to give it
meaning or energy.

And, while examining his hand sores: "All this
holy fierceness, for what, each forgotten sin?
Surely God has stopped counting."

Pilgrim's Gait

During his last Lent, as Anthony slept
on the first straw, giving his twitching tongue a rest,
the devil took to more: easing a slow constriction
around his throat, squeezing—so violently
that the accompanying sneer, inviting Anthony
to preach now, went unnoticed.

All the saint's words, gone—trying in vain
to speak Refuge. He could not get to saving words.
So he died, stopped a fight that was not his,
hand wrapping his mother—on a string.

And calm, always there, came to assure: a veil
about her working neck, a pail at her side.
He needed nothing. She touched his cheek,
gave a neckerchief sign on his forehead,
a smile which put the eternal refuse to flight
he can never escape.

Anthony closed his eyes, caught himself—
he wanted to turn for the win, to see
the pimpled arse; and that fluster, father
of all puffery, in his haste, obliged. Anthony's
small cell gleamed in angel voices, pillars,
the faces of heaven.

The pit of the pit had departed, too pathetic
even for comedy, confused, a little, at his
absurd fate—so far beneath him, and yet, not.

13. Concerning the Paduans' Devotion and the Results of His Preaching

Followers stopped whenever he did,
imitated his walk. In pewless churches,
surrounded by sweating statues, people surged,
clambered saints who helped in the reach—
all of heaven, closing for a hearing.

The Cathedral's doors opened too wide
to ever shut again, pushing Anthony,
what caused him, out to the first church: a meadow,
where privileged seats saved the poor.

People began to reclaim that city: streets
spelling childhood names. Castles crowned
perfect hills—like a brooch, while the next village
served on bended knee.

Before each dawn, talk began to populate
dark roads, a trail of candles burning
for stump and coming shade.

The old worked three legs—like holy spiders,
while the young veered, after new worlds.
Men and women of every turn, ornament, came,
some dressed as religious. The bishop
Iacopo di Corrad, all his clergy in amused tow,
sat next to his crozier, cross-legged in the dirt.

30,000 came, merchants, pulling wares.

Whatever was taken in the palsy, usury,
had to be returned; whoever had committed
mortgage placed the stolen money at his feet.
He loosed prostitutes from the hands
of their betters, thieves from hoarders.
Neither he nor the friars who followed
had hours enough to hear Confession.
People walked more slowly, after, as if
in pageant or conscious tableau. And after
his death, people confided that his apparition
had given them room and time on their road
for the speech of crickets.

He told them to enjoy the morning.

It would not come again.

14. How He Foretold His Own Death

Death saw right through him—
because he offered no resistance, so when
the final soft shoe neared, Anthony was already
there, among flowers that would rush him off.

He'd rest his head against a brother's back—
grapes falling off a bare table—walk Padua's plains,
feel them take him in: that fertility, so many seeds
in the air, yellow pollen, like the saints, you would
have thought the new world had already come.
It was a swarm of a city, more people than ideas,
hanging laundry. He liked that. Surely,
what it was meant to be would continue:
avenues of mercy.

The town housled Jesus in a tabernacle of trees.
Its shabby shingles made him weep.
Metaphor and more: his home, yes, it was
his dying bones, sinew as well.

Turning to friar Roger, Anthony stood
on his toes, told him simply that the town
would be honored: a rain of grace to sing green
the life it had been given, both now and later,
which was, of course, always now.

(His reshaping would be finished by then.
He would need something else to do!)

He did not intimate, and perhaps did not know
by whom the honor would come, nor upon
which citizens the grace would be conferred.

15. Concerning the Cell He Asked to be Built in the Nut Tree

The autumn harvest, fittingly, stopped him—
the rest, now, was someone else's concern.

Tiso, his heart torn real by the friars,
had given land enough to keep that need fresh;
each of their steps recalling all he had not done.

He wanted to hear that, always.

The man would offer new forest, its ways,
mazes, thick enough for contemplation. Yes!
Where a nut tree grew in a round—Biblical—
its trunk crowned by six stout horns, limbs:
like something out of Daniel, a fitting alleluia:
branches for the hiding of days.

Anthony was touched by the rough bark, the man;
climbed up on his last legs. (How much heaven
demanded, this ascent to God!) He wanted a cell
in that tree, half way up, to get him to nut stage:
provide a place where he could sing the Atlantic,
his incompleteness, home again.

Tiso prepared the bed of a cocoon, a floor of mats,
binding up saplings, the young lives they'd both

worn out in transversed branches. It was
the weave of God, as He made and unmade
every man's plans, taking, in the end, the person
himself; time closing up behind him.

Padua would weep.

Once in his cell, Anthony rejoiced, became one
with twining leaves, the birds, paying his last respects
in the breath that made him, to the earth
which had given him leave to dangle his feet
in salty air.

The Beat Catholic Line

–for Kerouac, Merton, Everson,
Levertov, Dylan, Berrigan, Cohen,
Springsteen, Mariani, Waits, Wright,
Daniels, and Karr

Prothalamion

> "I said shoot the gun, Weaver,
> and Weaver just laughin.'"
>
> Larry Craig

I.
Remember your ridiculous shag rug, brother, $600 delinquent:
"Let 'em come and rip it out. What are they going to do, wreck my credit?"
a leaning plywood audio stand, six junkers in the yard,
none of them running: you and all the low riders, West Side boys,
hot banjos, tool chests. Casey, hitting up all the crank he could feel
into his thumb, like Shirley wouldn't know he was off,
him circling our dining room, immersed,
by himself, in a three-way conversation.
A motorcycle would roar by. How he'd stop, look at me,
say, "Suzuki! . . . Yamaha! . . . Kawasaki?!" Then he'd grin.

I remember racks of clothes in the back seats of cars after work;
Jeff stealing all that shit from Zayre's on those overnighters:
an empty cookware box stuffed with jeans—four pair for nine bucks.
Convict Butch and his brother, that Chinese guy they said
they forced into their trunk: driving him around for three days,
pausing to take him out and talk it up; Danny, you, and Scotty

with your Sportsters. You cracking up with regularity, your back,
a sheet of juicy pink; Scotty letching because he couldn't reach out
to someone without pulling; Pat, proud of his genital length,
packing his guitar, speed, for a tow truck, nights on the interstate;
and at your house: Bob, still quaking from Army acid trips, Craig,
bound, determined to drink, to sail his way through the tomb.
Me and Fido, down through Quebec, into Maine, without pausing,
guards pulling us over, sure to find, she just knew, a seed.

73rd street boys. Remember those stacks—case after case of Miller
next to the fridge; spun tales of knocked off boxcars, how they'd busted
through the plywood in your door when you weren't home—
that picture of Jeff, standing half in, half out. When I asked them how
they'd managed it, they looked at me as if I were nuts: "Forklift."
Your twelve gauge, loaded in the closet, every one of you
to the stadium for a Billy Graham Crusade, getting saved and then,
within a week, back at it. Remember Mike writing to all those leather women
in a real, but faked, loneliness; Red, talking about how the doctor drained his arm
of hit-up downs, the fluid filling a small glass: him being shot five times in a bar,
slow motion, he said, like a hallucination. And Donna—her four abortions,
tripping since she was nine.

Downtown, near the college: Roman from next door: 1000 tuinals, pinball
wizards bouncing off apartment corridor walls; Danny's baseball friend,
tossing a radiator around in the hall; both Debbies, impromptu gigs
on pots and pans, guitars on 32nd. Debbie number one, past her bed, one bare
moon vying with the other: four guys and two women: one in the bathtub
with a soccer player, the other, on her ass, swishing up to me with her robe
opened to her golden triangle, the sound ringing in her semi-conscious head.

Then Butch killed Jeff, both of them speeding, shot him
because he wouldn't hand him the phone.

I walked night streets, tripping once in a college class—
sitting in the back, silent; it was the prof who freaked, broke class early:
my face pulling in different directions: comets inside skin, shooting, bouncing

off the pink insides, forcing occasional protrusions of the face,
the teeth grind, feeling metallic; cords in my stomach shook in waves,
like a bridge of bound, knotted bamboo shoots; the general body fuck;
how I felt fused, wanted to take off each limb, stick them into a garbage can
until they stopped quaking, twisting. I wanted to get rid of my teeth,
my brain, string my intestines like dried tripe from rock ledge to rock ledge.

The Jesus freaks drew me, their eyes, as I walked downtown to classes;
I'd go over to Pix's in my acid boots, having cut work, she and the baby
and Lee; or to the house of the wisest man I knew because Ginsberg
had suggested it. I talked about the wall's temporary nature, about how
they all have to come down. His wife rubbed her arms, left, and,
in a few minutes, he after her. I paced his room, Watched the dog watch me,
watched it piss on the carpet. I left, finally, rummaging more streets,
biding my time, waiting for a chance just to get out.

"You have not called me.
I have called you."

Jesus

II.
Even after my conversion—when I bussed it back to Steubenville,
for a Catholic university life; $45 in my pocket and a suitcase full of books,
night coming on. I knocked on rectory doors, a monastery finally
taking me in, thinking I was somebody else. There I found Hannah,
both of us, badly obedient, too much of the past closing in; God leading me away
to Redwood Valley, California. I abbey-sat: watched pigs, peacocks, chickens and sheep
for monks. Hugh, a disbarred lawyer showed up, writing bad fiction. And Rose,
ex-Hell's Angel, junkie prostitute, Indian princess. She took me to reservation
revivals: teeth being filled at the Grange Hall with gold, silver or pearl.
The preacher vilifying witches, saying God would raise the dead that Thursday!

An escaped killer from Soledad, acquaintance of the abbot, appeared
from some bushes one night—splitting later before cops, at 2 am, banged on
chapel doors; me, sleepy-eyed, looking at five pump shotguns.
I mourned for Hannah, the life I never got to, saw her broken
in my rosaries, dreams. When the monks returned, I headed back
to Steubenville, found Lida, re-formed lesbian, woman to my man:
my proposing three times, her accepting three times; she, dumping
all her man hate on me, and me, driving her into the army
with my furious wound, my self-contempt.

"No, not I, but Christ
who liveth in me."

St. Paul

III.
Brother, we are like weeds, having grown in the same field:
our arms, lettuce for the bees. As a kid, I used to watch you ride your bike,
standing on the seat into a fallen telephone pole, you diving, rolling
through the farmer's pumpkin patch. We have grown through the friends
and powers that have peopled our days. And now, Ragtime, another turning.
May it bring you peace—and children, realization that we are not here
for ourselves, but for the stubborn laying down, hands to wood,
feet to wood. And may the love that brought you, keep you, that boy aloft—
all the wars of Europe still moiling in his veins.

Last Acid

d. a. levy, acid eater, night pod, East Cleveland,

The cold made for walking: old brick buildings talking time and what it exacts:
a lifetime of punch clocks, dingy lunchrooms. Who wanted that?
Working for someone, giving him the rod and a carrot every Christmas.
A cabbie then? Maybe, grimy after long hours, alone with nothing to do
but sleep, playing the music of those pedals for weekends that never really came.

I followed you to Colorado. Me, Bill and Nancy to Rustic
in a '69 Tempest, hungry through turns, a hound after the bones of our delivery,
the two of them, funded, talking "the program," constructing a have attitude,
this thing they now believed in. I could take some smug, satisfaction
in being on the outside of that: people who wanted to forget everything
they hadn't learned—so they could write a better name. Did I want in?
Probably, but I didn't want to belong.

We rose through the sheer mountain rock, cliff faces—like Indians:
cross-hatched, red leather. Bill broke out the hash and we stopped, watched
the river speak itself, convex, rains pushing it toward apocalypse.

"F the program," I, aidless, said.

A year later, wanting to put some distance between me and Falwell,
I suggested peyote: praying at a night fire—where I felt it begin,
knotting my veins, a fist of life through stomach lining. Three of us
walked the salt road, me praying that the Starry Name might whiten us;

Tom eventually hiding in the arms of buffalo pine, calling out, lowing,
across the road, he and Bill, sitting in the dirt, lighting matches, talking sentience.
I lay down outside the circle, listened to the river turn its pages.

After twelve hours of prayer, virtual bliss, I began to come down,
wracked in the cabin, hearing leaves scuttle outside, over glossy animal
remains; the pocked white moon; my upper teeth dragged across gravel,
giving me the St. Vitas I, at times, still dance.

How would those bent teachers tend the night on Monday, I wondered,
how would they plump the cabbage?

And though, in the intervening years, d. a., in my own classrooms,
I've sometimes gotten the itch, career version: the one that makes me
feel like losing again, big-time, just to salvage a name I don't have,
just to lose the benefits, comfortable students and hack it again,
in East Cleveland, to exist in a world without politics, to curse those
whom I cut off (and the successful I don't: each one of those, holding
my attitude up for change); all so I could go back to a place, that,
because of the miles, could never be home, as real as my old boots,
as the artificial time the clock sweeps, me at 5 am, I haven't.

Because no matter how much I fight to try and make this about me,
it isn't. Here, in this closet of an office, I burn myself away, one student
at a time, in real life: ordinary service, every bit of youth gone
in a (sometimes) quiet conflagration.

My children, too, wax as I wane; my life, sticks to their fires.
I watch them burn, all the quiet rage each one stores, with a dad
who's come, sorry as we all are, to this: mixing memory with desire,
stirring dull roots, under a spring rain I, thankfully, do not bring.

Love at 2,700 Miles

—Puerto Rico

1.
At the foot of tourniquet foothills,
the scrubbed Colorado brush ascended
through red ash, pails of yellow grass;
distant mountains nodding,
brute chorus in the finite sun:
that work, that 99 degrees,
dried as hollowed bones
where we hauled up chunks of basement concrete
in five gallon buckets,
over shaft of window well,
bruised window frame, ran them,
two at time to the street.

At the lawn hose,
below magnetic hills, Living Water sprang up
from a tomb of cool purple cells,
fountains of rock and rib,
easing parchment earth.

Come out, I said.

2.
At week's end, the autumn sun still hot,
a cold one on the table,

I lay, gratefully spent, on the cool floor
next to the aquarium,
plaster still on my clothes, hands.

The Denver sky was an ornate blue,
a cooling breeze washed in.

Tears, I said, are the gifts a Lover brings.

3.
I would wait for You:
the past would drop like ocean's jewels
from my hands, the past would drop.
And all those misshapen stones, that tangled
jade green kelp would recede,
sea rings and fingers,
past the thin wet necklace,
would revolve in the belly of that blue turquoise,
beached whale.

Come, like new, Lord:
Your laughter over the Pacific,
Your gaze above the burning sea.

4.
Porch boards and hooks heaved and groaned.

From that swing, the sun, gone,
left its pink to walk the dark and settled roofs;
purple moved toward Golden
as pale stars torched the loose string
of sealed days.

5.
Here is that peace, today, in darkness,
where the passage of time is as falling leaves.

Here is the fizz in dark foam, duned prints,
here the gnarl of driftwood,
a white bird on a dark shore.

Notes

"Moment of Conscience"

The "moment" has been often prophesied. Everyone of earth will see their soul as God sees it. A painful, happy grace. But it will supposedly be too much for some, who will die during the experience. In the poem, the anticipated date turned out to be inaccurate.

"The Santa Fe Staircase (Tour)"

The original carpenters neglected to add stairs. As a result no one could get to the loft. The Sister of St. Joseph prayed to their protector, and a carpenter came, built them a miraculous one: thirty three tight steps, no rails, using skill not then available.

"Fake Apparition"

"Hoops" is basketball.

"1. Here Begins the Prologue"

In a children's book banned by Hitler, Ferdinand the bull likes to sit just quietly in the meadow, smelling the flowers.

"8. How his Learning was Noted by the Friars"

"Discovered and interrupted" is a phrase stolen from Beatrix Potter's "The Tale of Samuel Whiskers." The main character, a fat old rat, absconding with some food, is unexpectedly cut short of his goal. This is his response.